Bank Fraud

Wiley & SAS Business Series

The Wiley & SAS Business Series presents books that help senior-level managers with their critical management decisions.

Titles in the Wiley & SAS Business Series include:

Activity-Based Management for Financial Institutions: Driving Bottom-Line Results by Brent Bahnub

Bank Fraud: Using Technology to Combat Losses by Revathi Subramanian

Big Data Analytics: Turning Big Data into Big Money by Frank Ohlhorst

Branded! How Retailers Engage Consumers with Social Media and Mobility by Bernie Brennan and Lori Schafer

Business Analytics for Customer Intelligence by Gert Laursen

Business Analytics for Managers: Taking Business Intelligence beyond Reporting by Gert Laursen and Jesper Thorlund

The Business Forecasting Deal: Exposing Bad Practices and Providing Practical Solutions by Michael Gilliland

Business Intelligence Success Factors: Tools for Aligning Your Business in the Global Economy by Olivia Parr Rud

CIO Best Practices: Enabling Strategic Value with Information Technology, Second Edition, by Joe Stenzel

Connecting Organizational Silos: Taking Knowledge Flow Management to the Next Level with Social Media by Frank Leistner

Credit Risk Assessment: The New Lending System for Borrowers, Lenders, and Investors by Clark Abrahams and Mingyuan Zhang

Credit Risk Scorecards: Developing and Implementing Intelligent Credit Scoring by Naeem Siddiqi

The Data Asset: How Smart Companies Govern Their Data for Business Success by Tony Fisher

Delivering Business Analytics: Practical Guidelines for Best Practice by Evan Stubbs

Demand-Driven Forecasting: A Structured Approach to Forecasting, Second Edition, by Charles Chase

Demand-Driven Inventory Optimization and Replenishment: Creating a More Efficient Supply Chain by Robert A. Davis

The Executive's Guide to Enterprise Social Media Strategy: How Social Networks Are Radically Transforming Your Business by David Thomas and Mike Barlow

Economic and Business Forecasting: Analyzing and Interpreting Econometric Results by John Silvia, Azhar Iqbal, Kaylyn Swankoski, Sarah Watt, and Sam Bullard

Executive's Guide to Solvency II by David Buckham, Jason Wahl, and Stuart Rose

Fair Lending Compliance: Intelligence and Implications for Credit Risk Management by Clark R. Abrahams and Mingyuan Zhang

Foreign Currency Financial Reporting from Euros to Yen to Yuan: A Guide to Fundamental Concepts and Practical Applications by Robert Rowan

Health Analytics: Gaining the Insights to Transform Health Care by Jason Burke

Heuristics in Analytics: A Practical Perspective of What Influences Our Analytical World by Carlos Andre, Reis Pinheiro, and Fiona McNeill

Human Capital Analytics: How to Harness the Potential of Your Organization's Greatest Asset by Gene Pease, Boyce Byerly, and Jac Fitz-enz

Information Revolution: Using the Information Evolution Model to Grow Your Business by Jim Davis, Gloria J. Miller, and Allan Russell

Manufacturing Best Practices: Optimizing Productivity and Product Quality by Bobby Hull

Marketing Automation: Practical Steps to More Effective Direct Marketing by Jeff LeSueur

Mastering Organizational Knowledge Flow: How to Make Knowledge Sharing Work by Frank Leistner

The New Know: Innovation Powered by Analytics by Thornton May

Performance Management: Integrating Strategy Execution, Methodologies, Risk, and Analytics by Gary Cokins

Retail Analytics: The Secret Weapon by Emmett Cox

Social Network Analysis in Telecommunications by Carlos Andre and Reis Pinheiro

Statistical Thinking: Improving Business Performance, Second Edition, by Roger W. Hoerl and Ronald D. Snee

Taming the Big Data Tidal Wave: Finding Opportunities in Huge Data Streams with Advanced Analytics by Bill Franks

Too Big to Ignore: The Business Case for Big Data by Phil Simon

The Value of Business Analytics: Identifying the Path to Profitability by Evan Stubbs

Visual Six Sigma: Making Data Analysis Lean by Ian Cox, Marie A. Gaudard, Philip J. Ramsey, Mia L. Stephens, and Leo Wright

Win with Advanced Business Analytics: Creating Business Value from Your Data by Jean Paul Isson and Jesse Harriott

For more information on any of the above titles, please visit www.wiley.com.

Bank Fraud

Using Technology to Combat Losses

Revathi Subramanian

WILEY

Published by John Wiley & Sons, Inc., Hoboken, New Jersey.
Published simultaneously in Canada.

For general information on our other products and services or for technical support,
please contact our Customer Care Department within the United States at (800)
762-2974, outside the United States at (317) 572-3993 or fax (317) 572-4002.

Wiley publishes in a variety of print and electronic formats and by
print-on-demand. Some material included with standard print versions of
this book may not be included in e-books or in print-on-demand. If this book
refers to media such as a CD or DVD that is not included in the version you
purchased, you may download this material at http://booksupport.wiley.com.
For more information about Wiley products, visit www.wiley.com.

Library of Congress Cataloging-in-Publication Data

Subramanian, Revathi.
  Bank fraud: using technology to combat losses / Revathi Subramanian.
    Pages cm.—(Wiley & SAS business series; 25)
    ISBN 978-0-470-49439-4 (hardback)—ISBN 978-1-118-22032-0 (ebk)—
ISBN 978-1-118-23397-9 (ebk)   1. Banks and banking—Security measures.
2. Bank fraud—Prevention 3. Bank fraud—Prevention—Technological
innovation. I. Title.
  HG1616.S37S83 2014
  332.1068'4—dc23
                                                            2013046697

10 9 8 7 6 5 4 3 2 1

*To the amazing people who have
influenced me profoundly*

(given in chronological order of influence):

My parents, Srinivasan and Mahalakshmi

My brother Ramesh

My husband, Suresh

Contents

Preface xi

Acknowledgments xiii

About the Author xvii

Chapter 1   Bank Fraud: Then and Now   1
  The Evolution of Fraud   2
  The Evolution of Fraud Analysis   8
  Summary   14

Chapter 2   Quantifying Fraud: Whose Loss Is It Anyway?   15
  Fraud in the Credit Card Industry   22
  The Advent of Behavioral Models   30
  Fraud Management: An Evolving Challenge   31
  Fraud Detection across Domains   33
  Using Fraud Detection Effectively   35
  Summary   37

Chapter 3   In God We Trust. The Rest Bring Data!   39
  Data Analysis and Causal Relationships   40
  Behavioral Modeling in Financial Institutions   42
  Setting Up a Data Environment   47
  Understanding Text Data   58
  Summary   60

Chapter 4   Tackling Fraud: The Ten Commandments   63
  1. Data: Garbage In; Garbage Out   67
  2. No Documentation? No Change!   71
  3. Key Employees Are Not a Substitute for Good
     Documentation   75
  4. Rules: More Doesn't Mean Better   77
  5. Score: Never Rest on Your Laurels   79
  6. Score + Rules = Winning Strategy   83
  7. Fraud: It Is Everyone's Problem   85

8. Continual Assessment Is the Key   86
9. Fraud Control Systems: If They Rest, They Rust   87
10. Continual Improvement: The Cycle Never Ends   88
Summary   88

Chapter 5   It Is Not Real Progress Until It Is Operational   89
The Importance of Presenting a Solid Picture   90
Building an Effective Model   92
Summary   105

Chapter 6   The Chain Is Only as Strong as Its Weakest Link   109
Distinct Stages of a Data-Driven Fraud Management
   System   110
The Essentials of Building a Good Fraud Model   112
A Good Fraud Management System Begins with the Right
   Attitude   117
Summary   119

Chapter 7   Fraud Analytics: We Are Just Scratching the
            Surface   121
A Note about the Data   125
Data   126
Regression 1   128
Logistic Regression 1   132
"Models Should Be as Simple as Possible,
   But Not Simpler"   149
Summary   151

Chapter 8   The Proof of the Pudding May Not Be in the
            Eating   153
Understanding Production Fraud Model Performance   154
The Science of Quality Control   155
False Positive Ratios   156
Measurement of Fraud Detection against Account False
   Positive Ratio   156
Unsupervised and Semisupervised Modeling
   Methodologies   158
Summary   159

Chapter 9   The End: It Is Really the Beginning!   161

Notes   165

Index   167

Preface

I was introduced to the fascinating world of data-driven risk management back in the mid-1990s. Since then, I have come across repeated situations where the lack of planning of simple things resulted in a significant drop in the quality of the achievable, desired results. I felt that a book that detailed the steps of designing and implementing a data-driven risk management system—and how interconnected everything is—would really help practitioners of risk management achieve their goals. This book is aimed at helping business and IT users define their data and analysis environments correctly from the beginning so that the best possible results can be achieved by their risk (specifically fraud) management systems.

This book is not meant as a primer to convert the reader into a data scientist (that requires significant academic and practical training). Rather, it was written to help the reader become a power user of data-driven systems by covering in detail the ingredients necessary to build and maintain a healthy fraud management environment. Without the right data environment (and attitude of all the personnel involved), even the best, most advanced data-driven solutions cannot yield optimal results. *Bank Fraud: Using Technology to Combat Losses* aims to help define such an environment.

Acknowledgments

I would like to acknowledge the amazing pool of talent of analytic and business thought leadership that I have been associated with over the last two decades in the vibrant San Diego analytics community. Specifically, my mentor Krishna Gopinathan, who in my opinion is the father of data science. In the mid-1990s, when no company had thought of (much less succeeded in) commercializing artificial intelligence–based models for risk management, he created an environment at HNC Software that brought together the best minds from multiple deep applied science and engineering disciplines. This led to some world-class thinking and pioneered the use of sophisticated nonlinear techniques, such as neural networks, which he made the de facto standard across the world. The scientists he groomed at HNC have gone on to lead several large companies in data science, and they continue to influence the world of data-driven decisions greatly. This association has influenced my thinking very profoundly.

I would like also to acknowledge my mentor Lynn Wallis for the guidance he has given me in the business interpretation of deep analytics, which helps me organize my thoughts every day—his influence has shaped this entire book; T.J. Horan for his initial thoughts on the book chapters—he was supposed to co-author this book with me but couldn't, but if he had not agreed to write this book with me, I would not have even started on the path of writing it; Dr. Vijay Desai; Dr. Paul Dulany whose colorful interpretation of various analytical themes helped me greatly in explaining ideas; Dr. Vijay Desai, and Kannan Shah for helping me with the simulation using different techniques in Chapter 7. The ideas of Lynn, TJ, Vijay, and Paul are irretrievably intertwined with my analytical thinking and interpretation and I owe all of them special thanks.

I would like to acknowledge my husband, friend, philosopher, and guide, Suresh, for spending loads of time helping me organize and edit this book, for adding references, for keeping me encouraged and focused, and for his valuable initial feedback; my brother Ramesh for giving me the initial confidence and strength to write the book ("It is nothing, Revathi! Just a few interesting insights and few good examples and you will have the book done!") and cheering and pushing me periodically to make sure I completed it; my sisters-in-law Sudha and Ranjani for basically assuming that I had already completed the book (when I was less than halfway done with it) and talking about how to take it one step further and how to market it; my niece Sahana and sister-in-law Sujatha for assuming this book would get completed even when I had doubts; my parents for developing my many interests in multiple fields, for coaching and showing me by example that there is no substitute for hard work and for always believing in me; my second set of parents AKA my father-in-law and my mother-in-law for the pride and joy they take in all the time-consuming things I do including writing this book; my brother Ramesh and my good friend Shankar for impressing upon me the need to keep the book simple and engaging to read; my sons Akshai and Sanjai for being both amused by and enthused about this project; and my immediate family in San Diego for putting up with my already hectic schedule of work and travel that was rendered even more hectic over the last two years writing this book.

And I must again acknowledge my family and extended family—my sons Akshai and Sanjai; my husband, Suresh; my parents, Srinivasan and Mahalakshmi; my parents in-law, Ramachandran and Kalpakam; my brother Ramesh; my sisters-in-law Sudha, Sujatha, and Ranjani; my brothers-in-law Sukumar and Gopal; my nephews Shreyas, Varchas, and Sandeep; my nieces Smera, Medha, and Sahana; my goddaughter Sashi; and my aunts, uncles, cousins, friends: Lynn, Emily, TJ, Vijay, Paul, Hongrui, Srabani, Hema, Lalitha, Shankar, Seetha, Kalpana, Kiranavali, Jayasree, Vasanthi—thanks to them all for their tremendous loving support.

Also thanks to my current manager Rammohan Varadarajan for the encouragement he provided to help me wrap up the book; and my colleague Nat Natraj for his enthusiastic and valuable support.

I would like also to acknowledge the SAS Institute and, in particular, Dr. Jim Goodnight and David Park for their encouragement and support; also, Shelley Sessoms, Julie Platt, and Stacey Hamilton from the SAS Press team, and the team of reviewers at SAS, for all their support.

Thanks to John Wiley & Sons for the tremendous opportunity to write this book; my Editor, Sheck Cho, Editorial Coordinator Helen Cho, Director of Content assembly Emilie Herman, Developmental Editor Lia Ottaviano, and Senior Production Editor Natasha Andrews for their tremendous help in editing and making this book a reality.

About the Author

Revathi Subramanian is Senior Vice President, Data Science, at CA Technologies. She is the founding member of a team of high-caliber data scientists who are uncovering business value and operational intelligence from the chaos of big data in areas like eCommerce, application performance management, infrastructure management, service virtualization, and project management. CA Technologies helps Fortune 1000 companies manage and secure complex IT environments to support agile business services. Organizations leverage CA software and SaaS solutions to accelerate innovation, transform infrastructure, and secure data and identities, from the data center to the cloud. Revathi and her team are ushering in a new generation of innovative management capability by bringing together machine learning and CA's best-in-class data center management expertise, thus, giving CIOs powerful insights into their IT portfolios and enabling them to effectively manage large, complex data centers by transparently leveraging data science.

Before joining CA, Revathi was the co-founder of the SAS Advanced Analytic Solutions Division in 2002. She led the development of a new enterprise real-time fraud decisioning platform utilizing advanced analytics. Over the next ten years, she and her team added the name of SAS Institute to the world of real-time analytic solutions. Revathi helped establish SAS as one of the leading vendors in this space and is credited with multiple patents and some groundbreaking and innovative real-time scoring technology in fraud and risk management. Prior to joining SAS, Revathi held various leadership roles in HNC Software (which was acquired by FICO in 2002) and built highly innovative transaction-based credit risk, attrition risk, and revenue/profit forecasting systems. Right after graduate school, she was involved in research in orthopedic surgery and physical medicine as senior statistician at The Ohio State University hospitals. She also ran operations support for a local credit card company in Ohio.

While Revathi is very passionate about data science, she also has a number of other interests: carnatic music, travel, beadwork, cooking, and gardening. Revathi has a master's degree in statistics from The Ohio State University and a bachelor's degree in mathematics from Ethiraj College, Chennai, India.

CHAPTER 1

Bank Fraud: Then and Now

Perhaps the earliest recorded case of fraud in the Western world was that of Hegestratos and Xenothemis in 300 B.C.[1] The story goes that Hegestratos took out an insurance policy on a boat for a large sum, with the deliberate intention of sinking it. At this time, ships were going down at a very high frequency, so this was not necessarily a bad idea (from the point of view of the fraudster), provided one managed to pull it off. Hegestratos was supposed to carry a large amount of grain from Syracuse to Athens on his boat. His idea was to not carry any grain but sink the boat halfway through the voyage and collect the insurance money. He would get the price of the boat reimbursed, and since there was no grain on the boat, he wouldn't incur the loss of the value of the grain. What ended up happening was something else altogether. The people on the boat got wind of Hegestratos's plan to drown them and confronted him. Unable to face the opposition, Hegestratos jumped overboard and drowned himself. His partner, Xenothemis, had to sail the boat to the port, and things didn't go well for him either. A legal battle followed between the buyer, Protos, who was waiting in Athens, and Xenothemis, when Protos, who thought he was getting grain, found out that there was no grain on the boat.

Even though the exact details of the verdict in this legal battle are lost to history, we know that Hegestratos and Xenothemis were unable to carry out their plan, and things ended badly for both of them. While this is surely not the oldest case of fraud in history, it is one of the oldest *recorded* cases of fraud.

This chapter traces a rough history of fraud and compares the times we are in with historic times and looks at how complicated the world of fraud management has become. In order to begin laying the ground-work to understand how complex fraud detection systems have become a necessity in the last few decades, it is important to be aware of this history.

THE EVOLUTION OF FRAUD

If we look to the East, many stories of fraud exist in Hindu mythology and in the folklore of various parts of Asia. Fraud is probably as old as money itself, and we could go a step further and say that fraud has probably existed in this world for as long as human beings have inhabited it. One might ask, "What is different about the times we live in?" In historic times, unlike today, fraud was a rather sporadic phe-nomenon. There was also considerable stigma associated with fraud as most of it was discovered sooner rather than later, which served as a deterrent to its widespread use. Written over 2,500 years ago, the *Thirukkural*[2] is a masterpiece by the poet Thiruvalluvar composed of 1,330 couplets in the South Indian language Tamil (which happens to be my mother tongue). The 284th couplet says that the unbridled desire to defraud others, when fruitful, will produce endless pain and sorrow. This indicates that fraud existed many thousands of years ago, and most often it resulted in the fraudster reaping considerable noto-riety and sorrow. Not only was this the case in the East but also in the Western world, as evidenced in the Hegestratos and Xenothemis story.

Fraud in the Present Day

Fast forward to our times. Not only has fraud become much more pre-valent now compared to historic times, but the frequency and the ubiqui-tous nature of today's fraud means that fraudsters don't necessarily meet the end they deserve. Financial institutions are forced to fight fraud all the time. If fraud is not fought effectively, fraud losses can threaten to derail entire institutions. Some of this is because there are so many more human beings inhabiting the world today, and this results in interactions with institutions becoming more and more impersonal, thus opening up a rich environment for committing fraud. Fraudsters have become so sophisticated that they don't need to be present and make personal sacrifices like Hegestratos to carry out their plans. Fraud can be completely impersonal as far as the fraudsters are concerned.

Banks are especially vulnerable to fraud. Why are they so vulnerable? I am reminded of a conversation alleged to have occurred between Willie Sutton, a legendary and prolific bank robber, and a reporter, Mitch Ohnstad. Sutton is said to have robbed more than $2 million and spent over half of his adult life in prison. The reporter Ohnstad asked Sutton, "Why do you repeatedly rob banks?" to which Sutton replied, "Well, that is where the money is."[3] That statement pretty much sums up why banks are so popular with fraudsters. In most cases of fraud that banks experience, the fraudsters are never caught. All that the banks are able to do is to stop the bleeding by stopping fraud as soon as they can ; they have little hope of recouping the money lost.

In the good old days, when there were fewer customers and banks were for the most part local, they had the luxury of having face-to-face relationships with customers. In the last 40 or 50 years, this has been changing. Not only are there more and more (too many) customers to keep up with, but there also are many customers simply not available for face-to-face interactions. As banks got bigger and the pressure to get bigger and more profitable grew, they were forced to innovate in terms of customer acquisition as well as ways in which customers transact with the bank. As interactions with banks became more and more impersonal, the resulting anonymity also helped the fraudsters to exploit the system.

Risk and Reward

As we all know, lending money has been the business of banks almost from when they started. However, the amount of risk a bank is willing to take to lend money has changed dramatically in the last 50 years.

Gone are the days when customers had to appear personally at the banker's office and show the assets on which a loan is requested. In those days, not only were assets showing the customer's ability to pay back the loan needed, but there was also the need to have third parties assure the bank that the money would be paid back if the borrowing customer was unable to repay the loan.

Fast forward to 10 or 20 years ago: Pretty much anyone who had an account with the bank and the semblance of a job could walk in and get a loan—not secured, but an unsecured loan like a credit card and/or other types. Even though it seems to be a pretty risky path for banks to take, as long as they could manage the risk/reward equation by exercising decent control on the risk side, it became a very lucrative path for the banks. The reward portion of the equation is generally dictated by the volume of business a bank can generate. Most of the time, the volume of business is proportional to the number of customers. The same volume also helped fraudsters. The higher the number of customers, the more impersonal the relationships become. You can see how the continuum operates.

Secured Lending versus Unsecured Lending

Even with a rapidly growing customer base, it is possible to keep a decent amount of control on secured lending. In secured lending, there is an asset that the bank has control over that can be used to recoup losses it might incur, especially if the perpetrator is the customer. However, unsecured lending is a totally different beast. Unsecured lending is based on intangibles such as the behavior history of the customer and so on. In addition, since the customer does not have skin in the game, unsecured lending becomes a burden mostly on the bank. Unsecured lending pretty much opened the floodgates in terms of fraud. To a number of customers, it seemed like free money . . . almost. The biggest proliferation of unsecured lending happened in the area of credit cards. The concept of being able to get money using a small plastic card was not only an amazing idea, but also one that caused a lot of crooks to start thinking about how they could exploit this little plastic card to get the free flow of money going. Due to high interest rates for credit cards, in spite of the fraud losses, running credit card portfolios was and continues to be a very lucrative business for banks. However, if there was a way to control losses, credit card portfolios would be even more attractive for banks. This meant that issuers had to figure out a way to keep fraud losses in check. Various authentication methods such as signature matching were used in the beginning to keep fraud rates under control. Not surprisingly, fraudsters found easy ways around these authentication methods. This is when the realization came that studying the cardholders' behavior and looking for deviations would be a much more effective method of keeping fraud in check than using authentication methods, which the crooks could find ways around. Statistical models started do a better job of understanding the nuances of cardholder behavior and what is normal for a customer, so the automation of the process of detecting fraud as well as improved accuracy became a huge asset to managing fraud.

These days, interestingly, even authentication methods are expected to have some understanding of the customer beyond simply matching a password to the recorded password of the customer. We live in a complex world where customer expectations have grown, and as customers have become more sophisticated, there has been an inherent expectation that the banks should almost magically know the behavior of the customer based on past history.

In unsecured lending, a lot more diligence is needed in combating fraud because fraud directly affects the bottom line of banks, as there is no way to recover losses from the customers. About 15 years ago, the banks started to turn to systems based on technology. Some of these systems could see what the human eye could not. The human eye can see two dimensions and, with some help from the brain, can understand the third dimension. When we start thinking about higher dimensions and interactions, the human eye is simply incapable of seeing odd behavior. If you include the human intellect, it is possible to look a little further. However, no system is going to be as efficient and adept at finding fraudulent patterns that do not fit as statistical models. Technology had helped spearhead the phenomenon of interactions becoming more and more impersonal. Now the same technology (involving behavioral modeling) came to the rescue to address the problem it was partially responsible for creating.

Statistical Models and the Problem of Prediction

Yogi Berra, the legendary American baseball catcher and manager, once said, "It is hard to make predictions, especially about the future" (the predecessor to this statement was made by physicist Neils Bohr).[4] This very funny but very insightful quip applies to any prediction problem, and from one point of view, there is a lot of truth to this statement. As Nassim Nicholas Taleb, the author of the book *Black Swan,* says, it is true that vast portions of the future lie beyond our abilities to predict.[5] The same argument tends to get used quite a bit against statistical models as well. Since a significant portion of this book is aimed at detailing the evolution of data analysis and statistical modeling and how much both have helped in combating fraud, let me address this at the very beginning. From certain points of view, it might seem that statistical models are not adequate to accurately predict the future. However, from my point of view, statistical models for the most part do a great job of making good predictions about the future even when the predicted situation is not exactly the same as what was observed earlier. Statistical models are very good at limiting the exposure (or fraud risk) and giving us a decent handle on the future. Statistical models have a tremendous ability to understand complex patterns and extrapolate to a decent-sized region not only in but around the values that the models were trained on.

To put it in real terms, let's say that cash deposits of $10,000 or more followed by multiple withdrawals are risky. If a rule or a mathematical algorithm is written to monitor for cash deposits of $10,000 or more, it is simply incapable of seeing risk when a deposit of $9,000 is made followed by withdrawals. However, a statistical model can observe a $9,000 deposit followed by multiple withdrawals and flag the activity as risky even though the model has never seen the exact same type of activity in the data presented to it.

The key here is the proximity of the dollar figure to the original number, and it gets a lot more complex and hard to do as we move away from the number. Statistical models, though, afford us the ability to extrapolate and learn in regions previously unknown, as long as the regions are reasonably close to what has been observed earlier. In a way, this is the way the human race has managed to grow knowledge in any scientific field, isn't it? If you look to the field of medicine, the development of antibiotics was based on repeated scientific experiments where each scientific experiment relied on the previous one and slightly expanded the knowledge space. We learn from the accumulation of knowledge, experiment a bit, observe new results, gain knowledge, extrapolate slightly beyond our previous region of knowledge, and so on. Statistical modeling is no different. While there are certain areas in which the ability of statistical models is more limited than in others, today it is true that without risk management largely driven by statistical models with behavioral input, banks would not survive. This is a hard fact that stares at everyone whether or not one has affinity for statistical models.

There are many examples that have been provided almost since statistical models came into existence on how wrong these models can be. There are any number of jokes on confidence intervals and how little they mean. There is of course the famous (but often overused) statement, "There are three kinds of lies: lies; damned lies; and statistics," by British Prime Minister Benjamin Disraeli, which was popularized by Mark Twain.[6] As much of a lover of statistics that I am, I would go one step further and say that the one thing you can be sure of with any statistical prediction is that it is not precise. When I say that a transaction's fraud score is 930 (meaning a probability of fraud of 0.93), the one thing we know for sure is that it is not correct. The transaction is either fraudulent or not, which should lead to a score of 0 or 1,000, translating to a probability of 0 or 1 if we simply want to be precise. But most fraud scoring systems do not use the score 0 or 1,000. Does this mean that fraud scoring systems are not useful? Absolutely not! When it comes to statistics, it is important to focus on how useful the output of a model is rather than whether the exact prediction is right or wrong. A score prediction is expected to be right in a large enough set of transactions with the same score, not for an individual transaction. Life is never about the extremes. It is always about the shades of gray that we need to understand more clearly.

So, while there have been countless number of writers before me and I am sure there will be countless number of writers after me who readily talk about the imprecise nature of statistical models, the benefits a statistical model provides are not as much in its precision and accuracy as it is in the rank ordering it provides. As long as a score of

930 has a much higher probability of fraud compared to a score of 850, a ton of value can be gained from the score, especially in high-volume areas where there is a need to separate the goods from the bads very quickly. In an environment where thousands of transactions are queuing up every second for a decision, it is important to quickly categorize transactions into groups with various false positive rates so that analysts' time can be well spent on identifying fraud. To this end, statistical models work wonders.

Also, it is important to understand that while the individual score of 930 may not be precise for a single transaction, if enough transactions with the score of 930 are accumulated, in the group, overall, the score could be calibrated such that 93 percent of the transactions would be fraudulent. In some ways, this is as precise as life gets! So, next time, before we criticize a statistical model for its imprecision at the very granular level, we should try to understand at a high level what the model is trying to do and what the practical use of the model is. We can then appreciate the amazing contributions from statistics that make our lives a lot easier.

Almost every technique and every advance in technology has its pros and cons. What we should look at in evaluating anything is to see if it directionally improves and advances our understanding of what is going on. This is the most important way to look at any scientific advancement. Statistics has been at the receiving end of more than its fair share of notoriety and ridicule of its shortcomings and issues. However, if statistical models are evaluated (with all their limitations, of course) from the point of view of how effective they have been in combating fraud, the wonders that have been possible in the area of fraud management can be appreciated. This evolution holds true for a number of different industries, but this book mostly focuses on modeling as applied to bank fraud. With this said, let's look at how things evolved in the banking industry.

THE EVOLUTION OF FRAUD ANALYSIS

Back in the good old days, when most banking was personal and most of the authentication was personal too, fraud could be handled very well. If the only way you can withdraw money is by walking into a bank and having a teller check your identity, it is a lot harder for someone to take over your identity and commit fraud. Enter the age of impersonal banking where transactions can be conducted from anywhere. It became necessary to see only the signatures of the people transacting without really seeing them face to face, as customers did not have to be available in person.

Early Credit Card Fraud

Building these customer signatures is a process of evolution that is easy to observe in the area of unsecured lending in the financial industry. Take credit cards, for instance. Twenty years ago, when credit cards were proliferating and everyone wanted to get one, and every bank wanted to sign up as many customers as possible for their credit cards, the banks had a real problem on their hands. Pre-set spending limits (typically in the many thousands of dollars) were imposed on customers, but when a credit card was lost accidentally by the customer or was stolen, fraudsters had free rein for a few days while the banks were literally robbed of the unspent credit line. The banks couldn't do a whole lot to stop it, as neither the customer nor the bank had a clue that fraud was being committed. Add to this the lack of liability on the part of the consumer. In order to limit consumer exposure, laws were passed. Consumers by law were not liable for more than $50 or so, and the banks were stuck with the lion's share of the losses. Necessity is the mother of invention, they say. The first seeds of the need for some heavy-duty technology were being sown then and there.

Fraud departments in those days were mostly staffed with ex–security personnel. These experts had a pretty good idea of what to look for in transactions on a transaction-by-transaction basis and started collecting data and writing reports to understand the nature of the fraud they were dealing with. Data collection and reporting certainly shed a lot of light on the nature of the fraud problem, but by the time experts saw what was going on, it was typically too late to do anything to stop fraud. It was like looking in the rearview mirror while driving a car and simply understanding what had happened already. The bleeding had occurred, and even though fraud losses in general were only a few basis points (as opposed to credit risk [delinquency] losses, which ran in the hundreds of basis points), fraud losses were beginning to take a tremendous toll on the psyches as well as the pocketbooks of many banks.

Once reports were written to analyze the data and understand what was going on, some of the more number-savvy fraud analysts and managers started seeing correlations between various quantities. For instance, they began to see that fraudsters prefer committing fraud at night. They also figured out that fraudsters like to check out whether the card had any credit line left by doing some small-dollar charges at a terminal far enough away from a watchful human eye so as to reduce the chances of getting caught in the first fraudulent transaction they were committing. Once the fraudsters figured out there was money available in the card and the card was still working, they tried to do as many fast transactions as possible such that the goods purchased in these transactions could be converted to easy money. For example, buying jewelry or purchasing electronic goods fetched money a lot faster than buying books.

When fraud experts at banks saw that most fraudulent transactions had a certain set of characteristics and some of the quantities they saw varied proportionally to certain other quantities that they had observed, they decided that they would start writing some rules to tackle the fraud. For example, let's say electronics store purchases are risky, but they are even more risky if the purchases are happening at night. One could write a rule that says that if the purchase is at an electronics store and it happens at night close to the time the store is closing, that transaction needs to be blocked right away so that the money flow can be stopped.

Separating the Wheat from the Chaff

This worked for a very short period, and then things didn't go as expected. Consumers had started using credit cards much more than they previously had for two reasons. First, consumers realized that using a credit card is really free money for an average of 45 days (on average, it takes 15 days for transactions to show up on the monthly bill, and the customer has an additional 30 days to pay off the bill) if they had the discipline to pay their bills every month. Second, consumers realized that while they were responsible for paying the minimum amount due every month, they really didn't have liability when it comes to fraud; all they had to do was call the bank and ask to cancel the card and get a new card issued. If the bank hesitated, the consumers could always just respond to the multitude of credit card offers hitting their mailboxes every week and get brand-new cards. All of a sudden, there were legitimate customer purchases happening late at night at electronics stores. Stopping all electronics store transactions also meant that the revenue from these transactions could not be realized by the banks. Just as fraud losses needed to be controlled, the revenue side of the equation also needed to be managed. From the customers who transacted heavily, as opposed to carrying a balance and interest (also known as revolving), the main source of revenue for the banks was interchange revenue. Stopping all those high-dollar transactions meant a significant loss in interchange revenue. The problem of separating the wheat from the chaff in terms of fraud had just become more difficult. Plus, the customers were getting more demanding in terms of treatment. They were not very pleased if their genuine transaction at night was misidentified as fraudulent (a "false positive") and stopped. The customers demanded that the bank figure out which transactions were real and which ones were not.

When a large quantity of data is analyzed and some simple correlations are observed through reports, it is literally like lighting a candle or turning the light bulb on in a dark room. A lot of value in the insight is gathered, and experts start to observe when things are going wrong, to the extent that these patterns can be observed and understood by the human eye and intellect. There are a couple of problems, though. As in the rearview mirror example I mentioned earlier, you can understand what has already happened, but that in itself doesn't prevent issues in the future. These lessons need to be converted to proactive decisions that can be made in the future. And the understanding itself is rather limited, and these limitations have to be overcome in order for the lessons to be used effectively in preventing fraud in the future.

The Advent of Nonlinear Statistical Models

Simple statistical models such as linear and logistic regression models are much better at understanding and generalizing fraud versus non-fraud behavior compared to expert-written rules. All of the variables that might have an impact on detecting fraud can be used as variables in the models. With respect to interactions between the different variables in the model, as long as the experts are able to figure out the interactions and feed them as variables into the model, the models are capable of understanding the behavior and its relationship to fraud. Unfortunately, experts don't have an infinite amount of time to understand and code these variables. For this reason, the simple statistical models started giving a huge number of false positives, and as the fraudsters got more sophisticated, neither rules nor simple models could be used to stop fraud effectively.

This was happening around the time that unsecured lending was proliferating at a very rapid pace. The income prospect for banks in unsecured lending was significant, and banks couldn't grow without it. These were the days when it was relatively common to receive a dozen credit card offers in the mail in any given month. As credit cards began to take off, credit card fraud losses began to increase drastically as well. The need to control fraud risk was real, as fraud losses could literally make or break the bank's profit numbers for that quarter.

It was at this time that some advanced nonlinear statistical models were introduced that could score transactions in real time to detect fraud. Nonlinear models like neural networks have the ability to understand and include interactions between various types of behaviors automatically. Most risk phenomena are nonlinear in their relationship to the target, especially something like fraud that is quickly changing as fraudsters get more and more sophisticated. The use of neural network–based behavior models in real time literally has changed the face of fraud management all over the world. It significantly reduced banks' fraud exposure in areas where there is a need to react in a split second and stop the transaction before money goes into the hands of the fraudster. When we examine how a credit card– or debit card–based transaction happens at a merchant point of sale (POS) terminal, we will realize that the bank has only several milliseconds to make the approve-or-decline decision on the transaction.

For instance, say a customer is at the POS terminal trying to purchase electronics worth $1,000. The bank has just seconds to decide whether to approve or decline the transaction. Considering the amount of time it takes to send the decision back to the host system and so on, the amount of time available purely to make the fraud decision is on the order of milliseconds. So, not only do we need sophisticated models that compare current behavior to past behavior and quickly judge using a model whether this transaction is fraudulent, it is also necessary for this model to run extremely fast in production systems.

The production execution of the model has to be precise (from a fraud-detecting perspective) and extremely fast in terms of returning an answer. When systems that could accomplish both of these objectives were first introduced in the marketplace, almost overnight the impact to fraud losses was huge. All of a sudden, the fraud problem could be tackled very effectively. Not only did this have an extremely positive effect on managing fraud, but in a lot of ways these systems paved the way for the tremendous growth in unsecured lending that in turn led to the growth of banks. Data-driven fraud detection systems have had a transformational effect on the banking industry.

Tackling Fraud with Technology

We have not yet seen the best of what can be done using behavioral modeling, not only in the area of fraud but in decision making in a number of customer touchpoints. In terms of advertisement monetization and a number of other areas, the fun with behavioral models is just beginning. In the next few decades, I predict that the world is going to witness, in a very broad sense, the impact that understanding data, modeling the data, and predicting the future will have on every decision made by institutions that requires customer insight.

In order to understand the use of technology in tackling bank fraud, we should perhaps start with the evolution of predictive modeling as a field and understand the evolution of statistics and data analysis techniques. Statistics is considered to have been born along with cryptography, based on the ninth-century book by Al-Kindi titled *Manuscript on Deciphering Cryptographic Messages*.[7] In this book Al-Kindi gives a detailed description of how to look at data frequencies to decipher cryptographic messages. Observing numbers and analyzing their natural frequencies provide a lot of information on whether they are following a certain pattern or not.

SUMMARY

In this chapter, we examined how fraud has evolved since historic times and how the nature of fraud has changed at a very rapid pace in the last couple of decades. The need for sophisticated nonlinear statistical models was also well established.

Over the next several chapters, we will examine the evolution of technology in the area of fraud detection, the challenges from an operational perspective, and how the future of risk management is looking really bright, due not only to current techniques but also to techniques that are very promising but have yet to be used in risk management specifically. I hope the reader has found this time travel interesting and informative.

CHAPTER **2**

Quantifying Fraud: Whose Loss Is It Anyway?

onsidering the long history of banking and the need to manage funds and fraud, fraud detection using data analysis is a relatively recent phenomenon. However, the growth in this area has followed a trajectory similar to the trajectory of technology in general but perhaps with a lag in start time. Back in the late 1980s when I immigrated to the United States, I didn't know what a computer looked like. Now my life and the lives of everyone around me are irrevocably interwoven with the digital world. Could anyone have imagined the kind of impact computers would have on our day-to-day lives today even as late as 25 years ago? Isn't it amazing how far we have come?

If we look at the use of data not just from the point of view of understanding what has happened in the past but from the perspective of using the data to decide what can be done in the future, I would say the use of data is still somewhat limited. If we look at the proliferation of data in this world, it is moving at a much faster rate than computers have in the past few decades. The executive chairman of Google, Eric Schmidt, said, "I spend most of my time assuming the world is not ready for the technology revolution that will be happening to them soon."[1] I believe that we actually haven't seen all that much yet; the best is yet to come.

This chapter examines the origin of credit and debit cards (which still are a very significant portion of a bank's fraud numbers) and challenges involved in the seemingly simple task of discovering where fraud has occurred. This important first step, if done well, would yield excellent results, though it is possible to get excellent results even when no past fraud info is available. This is because modern modeling technology can use sophisticated techniques that rely on nonlinear anomaly detection to deal with such cases.

Data Storage and Statistical Thinking

By many known accounts, we produce and store more data in a day now than mankind did altogether in the last 2,000 years. The data that is produced on a daily basis is estimated to be one exabyte, which is the computer storage equivalent of one quintillion bytes, which is the same as one million terabytes. Not too long ago—about 15 years—a terabyte of data was considered to be a huge amount of data. I remember, a few years ago, the first time a team I was on managed to get one terabyte of space on our servers for a project and the number of levels of approval that were required to acquire this. We were literally dancing in the hallways when we managed to get one terabyte of disk space purchased. I also remember the sense of accomplishment we felt when we finally got to play with the additional disk space. Fast forward to today—I was reading a few days ago that the latest Swiss Army knife comes with a 1-terabyte flash drive![2]

Data storage has become less and less expensive and hence is more and more accessible to everyone. Companies have spent billions of dollars acquiring storage space and organizing information in the form of data. The next several decades are going to be dominated by the systematic use of this information to make better decisions at all levels. Statistical thinking will be an essential ingredient to living.

I am reminded of and completely agree with what H. G. Wells said: "Statistical thinking will one day be as necessary a qualification for efficient citizenship as the ability to read and write."[3] This day is not far away, if not already here. I strongly believe and predict that statistics will play a very vital role in all walks of life and all day-to-day business interactions. Statistics and predictive modeling specifically are already playing a role in a number of our interactions, but the role is not a very visible one. Also, I suspect that statistical models are not being used as effectively as they could be.

The use of this science in the form of behavioral modeling is going to be very pronounced in certain interactions in the future. The interactions we have with our banks are going to be dominated by statistical thinking and predictive models in the future.

Understanding Non-Fraud Behavior

When an interaction with a business is complete, the information from the interaction is only as good as the pieces of data that get captured during that interaction. Let's say we walk into a bank and withdraw cash. The transaction that just happened gets stored as a monetary withdrawal transaction with certain characteristics in the form of associated data. There might be information on the date and time when the withdrawal happened; there may be information on which particular customer made the withdrawal if there are multiple customers who operate the account. The amount of cash that was withdrawn, the account from which the money was taken out, the teller/ATM who facilitated the withdrawal, the balance on the account after the withdrawal, and so forth, can be recorded. These are just a few data elements that get captured in a withdrawal transaction. Just imagine all the different interactions possible on all the different products that a bank has to offer: checking accounts, savings accounts, credit cards, debit cards, mortgage loans, home equity lines of credit, brokerage, and so on. The data that gets captured during all these interactions goes through data-checking processes and gets stored.

The data that gets stored this way has been steadily growing over the past few decades, and, interestingly, most of this data carries tons of information about the nuances of the customers' normal behavior.

In addition to what the customer does, from the same data, by looking at a different dimension of the data, we can also understand what is normal for certain other entities. For example, by looking at all the ATM withdrawals at a particular ATM from the customers of a particular bank, we can gain a good understanding of what is normal for the ATM terminal.

Understanding the normal behavior of customers is very useful in detecting fraud since deviation from normal behavior is a huge indicator of fraud. Understanding non-fraud or normal behavior is not only important at the main account holder level but also at all the entity levels associated with the account. The same data presents completely different information when observed in the context of one entity versus another. In this sense, having all of the data saved and then analyzing and understanding it is a key element to tackling the fraud problem. We will look at this in more detail in the next chapter. In this chapter, let's look at the main phenomenon we are discussing, namely fraud. Understanding and quantifying fraud in banking can be quite tricky due to a number of reasons.

Quantifying Potential Risk

Any systematic, numbers-based system of understanding the phenomenon of fraud as it happened in the past is dependent on an accurate description of what happened through the data that got accumulated before, during, and after the fraud episode occurred. Allowing the data to speak is the key to the success of any model-based system. This data needs to be saved and interpreted very precisely in order for the models to make sense. The first important step to building a model is to define, understand, and interpret fraud correctly. At first glance, this seems like a very easy problem to solve. Actually, in practical terms, it is a lot more difficult than it seems.

Philip Stanhope, a British statesman who lived in the 18th century, once made an interesting statement in a different context. He said, "It is always right to detect a fraud, and to perceive a folly; but it is very often wrong to expose either. A man of business should always have his eyes open, but must often seem to have them shut."[4] Sometimes I wonder if the financial institutions follow this idea of not exposing fraud even within the institution! The level of understanding of the fraud episode itself varies greatly among the different departments dealing with different products within the bank. Typically, fraud has a huge impact on the bottom line of the banks. However, if we look at the level of information that is systematically stored and analyzed about fraud in financial institutions, one would arrive at the conclusion that it needs to be a lot more rigorous than it is today. There are a number of factors influencing this.

Unlike some of the other types of risk involved in banking, fraud risk is a censored problem. For example, if we are looking at serious delinquency, bankruptcy, or charge-off risk in credit card portfolios, the actual "dollars-at-risk" quantity is very well understood. Based on past data, it is relatively straightforward to quantify precise credit risk dollars at risk by looking at how many customers defaulted on a loan or didn't pay their monthly bill for three or more cycles or declared bankruptcy. Based on this, it is easy to quantify the amount at risk as far as credit risk goes. However, in fraud, it is virtually impossible to quantify the actual amount that would have gone out the door as the fraud is forced to stop soon after action is taken. The problem is censored as soon as some intervention takes place, and it is hard to quantify the potential risk.

Recording the Fraud Episode

Another challenge in the process of quantifying fraud is how well the fraud episode itself gets recorded. Let's take the case of a credit card number getting stolen without the physical card getting stolen. This type of fraud is currently very common. Gone are the days when fraudsters needed the physical card to withdraw money. Now all that the fraudsters need is some semblance of detail on the card, and they can try all possible numbers on an Internet site and create the specific cards that allow them to transact. Back to an earlier example—let's say that for a certain period, both the legitimate cardholder and the fraudster were charging using the card. If the fraud detection system in the bank did not identify the fraudulent transactions as they were happening, typically fraud is identified when the cardholder gets the monthly statement and figures out that some of the charges were not made by him/her. Then the cardholder calls the bank to report the fraud. For a long time, all that used to get recorded by the bank was the cardholder's estimate of when the fraud episode began, even though there were details about the fraudulent transactions that were likely shared by the cardholder. If all that gets recorded is the cardholder's estimate of when the fraud episode began, it leads to ambiguity in terms of the actual fraud episode. The estimate of the fraud amount also becomes a rough estimate at best.

In the case where the bank's fraud detection system was able to catch the fraud during the fraud episode, the fraudulent transactions are recorded by the fraud analyst, and this may not be accurate. If the transaction were marked as fraud or non-fraud incorrectly, this is typically not corrected even after the correct information flows in. When eventually the transactions that were actually fraudulent are identified using the postings of the transactions, relating this back to the authorization transactions is not a straightforward process. Sometimes the amounts of the transactions may vary slightly. For example, the authorization transaction of a restaurant charge is unlikely to include the tip that the customer added to the bill. The posted amount when this transaction gets reconciled would look slightly different from the authorized amount. All of this poses an interesting challenge when designing a data-driven system to combat fraud.

The level of accuracy associated with recording fraud data also tends to be dependent on whether the fraud loss is a liability for the customer or the bank. To a large extent, the answer to the question "Whose loss is it?" really drives how well past fraud data is recorded. In the case of unsecured lending such as credit cards, most of the liability lies with the banks, and the banks tend to care a lot more about this type of loss. Hence systems are put in place to capture this data on a historical basis reasonably accurately. In the case of secured lending, ID theft, and so on, a big portion of the liability is really on the customer, and it is up to the customer to prove to the bank that he or she has been defrauded.

Interestingly, this shift of liability also tends to have a huge impact on the data quality of the fraud data captured. In the case of fraud associated with automated clearing house (ACH) batches and domestic and international wires, the problem is twofold: The fraud instances are very infrequent, making it impossible for the banks to have a uniform method of recording frauds; and the liability shifts are dependent on the geography. Most international locations put the onus on the customer, while in the United States there is legislation requiring banks to have fraud detection systems in place. The extent to which the banks take responsibility also tends to depend on how much they care about the particular customer who has been defrauded. When a very valuable customer complains about fraud on the account, a bank is likely to pay attention. Given that most frauds are not large scale, there is less need to establish elaborate systems to focus on and collect the data and keep track of past.

The past fraud information is also influenced heavily by whether the fraud is third-party or first-party fraud. Third-party fraud is where the fraud is committed clearly by a third party, not the two parties involved in a transaction. In first-party fraud, the perpetrator of the fraud is the one who has the relationship with the bank. The fraudster in this case goes to great lengths to prevent the banks from knowing that fraud is happening. In this case, there is no reporting of the fraud by the customer. Until the bank figures out that fraud is going on, there is no data that can be collected. Also, fraud could go on for quite a while and some of it might never be known. This poses some interesting problems. Internal fraud where the employee of the institution is committing fraud could also take significantly longer to find. Hence the data on this is scarce as well.

Supervised versus Unsupervised Modeling

All of the factors discussed above play a role in how well the data is recorded. When the fraud information is poorly recorded, it limits the extent to which target-based or supervised modeling can be done. In supervised modeling, there is a clearly defined target that you are trying to predict using independent variables as opposed to an unsupervised modeling methodology where there are no known or recorded past examples of the behavior you are attempting to predict.

In a semi-supervised modeling methodology, there are some known examples of the fraud behavior from the past, but not all of them. The unsupervised and semisupervised methods focus on cases where there is limited information about the fraudulent behavior. The good news is that there are very effective methods to understand aberrant behavior even with limited past examples of fraud, but the results are far superior in modeling methods that have known examples of fraud used to train the model. Hence, it makes a lot of sense for banks to capture fraud information very diligently, record the information, and make the information available to future modeling exercises.

The Importance of Accurate Data

Getting fraud data accurately captured, categorized, and stored is the first important step to using data-driven technology to combat fraud losses. This might seem very easy but, on close examination, we will figure out very quickly that having fraud data stored reliably over a long period of time requires a systematic approach at all levels at the bank. The idea of any piece of data being important to addressing a problem is a relatively new concept in the history of banking.

Accumulating accurate data starts with an overall vision of how the multiple steps in the process connect and affect the outcome. It is important for every member of the team to understand how important each step is in capturing the information correctly—from the person who is responsible for risk management in the bank to the people who run the fraud analytics department to the person who designs the data layout to the person who enters the data. A customer service analyst or a fraud analyst not marking a transaction correctly as fraud does have an impact on developing an accurate fraud system. Sometimes it really helps to establish rigorous processes of data entry and explain why the processes are in place. Process without communication and communication without process both are unlikely to produce desirable results. In order to understand the importance of recording fraud information correctly, it is important to understand how a data-driven detection system (whether it is based on simple rules or on sophisticated models) is developed.

FRAUD IN THE CREDIT CARD INDUSTRY

Fraud management in banks has become an extremely complex task. Whenever I think of the challenge fraud risk managers face, the analogy I think of is the one a longtime associate, Dr. Paul Dulany, told me—that of King Sisyphus from Greek mythology. Even though I was already aware of King Sisyphus, I took a keen interest in learning about him after hearing this analogy. King Sisyphus was the founder and ruler of Corinth. He was known to be one of the most cunning kings who had ever walked the earth. He was so clever that he managed to lock Hades, the god of death, in a closet in his house. This caused tremendous havoc in the world. No one could die. Even people badly hurt in battles managed to survive but suffered broken limbs and serious injuries. Hades was finally released and King Sisyphus was ordered to report to the underworld for his eternal assignment. Sisyphus tried to play a few more tricks along the way, but his misdeeds caught up with him at the end.

When he finally reached the underworld, his assignment was to roll a great boulder to the top of a hill. Every time Sisyphus managed to take the boulder all the way up to the top of the hill, the boulder would roll back down again. This is going on to this day in the underworld, according to Greek mythology. Fraud management in banks is also a Sisyphean task as it, too, is never ending. However, the good news for fraud managers is that their task is more interesting than what Sisyphus is enduring in the underworld. What one needs to do to tackle fraud effectively keeps changing as the nature of fraud keeps on changing. The challenge is there, but it is far from monotonous.

For the purpose of illustrating the changing nature of fraud, let's take the example of credit and debit card fraud. This can be big in dollar terms. Some other categories of fraud, like check fraud, tend to be large in value as well, but I would say that fraudsters have been much more innovative and creative in the area of card fraud. Card fraud is one area where you can clearly demonstrate the changing nature of fraud. Let's look at the evolution of card fraud over the last 30 years.

Early Charge and Credit Cards

In order to look at the evolution of fraud in the card industry, we should look at the evolution of credit cards. According to the paper titled "Credit Card and Payment Efficiency" by Stan Sienkiewicz of the Federal Reserve Bank of Philadelphia,[5] proprietary charge cards started in the early 1900s; they were followed by travel and entertainment cards in the 1950s. These cards were not truly credit cards as they did not have a revolving credit feature. The predecessor to credit cards was possibly the Charge-It card issued in 1946 by John Biggins, a banker in Brooklyn. When a customer used the card and made a purchase, the bill was sent to the bank. The bank acted as the intermediary, paid the merchant, and then got reimbursed by the cardholder. This card restricted the purchases to just local purchases. In 1951, New York's Franklin National Bank issued a card for loan customers, and it could only be used by customers of the bank. This was followed by Diners Club cards. These were small cardboard cards and mainly used for travel and entertainment. Diners Club had 20,000 or so customers within a couple of years. In the 1960s, the cardboard cards were replaced with plastic cards. Even though Diners Club cards could be used to make purchases on credit, the entire bill was due at the end of the month. So, it was really a charge card and not a credit card.

American Express, a giant in credit cards now, was formed in the mid-1800s. At that time, it was a competitor to the U.S. Postal Service and also offered money orders and traveler's checks. Traveler's checks were American Express's contribution to the financial industry—they invented the concept. Even though American Express apparently had discussed a travel charge card before Diners Club issued its charge cards, American Express was behind Diners Club. The American Express celluloid charge card for travel and entertainment was introduced in 1958 and was purple in color. The next year, it introduced plastic cards. American Express was probably the first company to have a massive international presence in credit cards. About one million cards were being used in about 85,000 establishments in the first five years. According to Sienkeiwicz, both American Express and Diners Club were closed-loop systems, made up of the consumer, the merchant, and the issuer of the card. In a closed-loop system, the issuer authorizes as well as handles all aspects of the transaction and settles directly with the consumer and the merchant. In 1959, the ability to maintain a revolving balance was available to customers.

According to the article "The History of Credit Cards" by Ben Woolsey and Emily Starbuck Gerson,[6] the first true general-purpose credit cards were issued in 1966 by Bank of America. Bank of America established the BankAmerica Service Corporation (this later became Visa) that franchised the brand nationwide. With this, other banks started issuing general-purpose credit cards as well. A national credit card system was formed when a group of banks got together and formed the InterBank Card Association (ICA). The ICA evolved into MasterCard (for some time this was known as MasterCharge). As the number of banks interested in issuing credit cards grew, they became members of the MasterCard association or the Visa association. By sharing the cost of running the program, even small financial institutions could afford to issue credit cards. Initially, credit card–issuing banks could belong to only one of the two associations. Later on, the bylaws of the associations changed to allow banks to issue cards through both associations. A single bank could issue both credit cards affiliated with Visa and MasterCard to their customers. The system used by Visa and MasterCard was an open-loop system where the transaction data was shared with all the members. Visa and MasterCard at first enjoyed an exclusive relationship with the banks for issuing cards.

As the number of credit cards issued increased, the associated processing became more complex. There were some external companies that started selling processing services. The processing companies used economies of scale to reduce the effort and cost involved in issuing cards, paying merchants for the transactions, and then settling in turn with the cardholders. This caused a very interesting expansion in the whole industry. For the smaller banks, issuing credit cards did not have a huge start-up cost of processing anymore. This started the tremendous expansion of credit cards. First Data Corporation, which started out as Mid-America Bankcard Association (MABA), is probably one of the oldest such processing companies.

In the mid-1990s, there were many small banks with a few million credit cards each. Significant consolidation has taken place in the market since the early 2000s, when a number of smaller credit card portfolios were bought out by larger issuers and a few really large issuers emerged. Partly due to this, in the last decade, many banks have gone through the cycle of using a processor for a few years and then taking the processing in-house for a few years and then going to a processor again for a few years. This has also had significant impacts on the quality and quantity of data available.

American Express was one of the first companies to issue charge cards. However, it issued its first true credit cards only in 1987. Though its initial focus was travel and entertainment cards, the company has now developed a number of no-annual-fee credit cards, very similar to bank cards. Discover introduced its first credit card in 1986. Discover also created its own merchant network, which is among the largest networks in the world now. After a 2004 ruling, Discover and American Express cards were also allowed to be issued by banks. Since this ruling, Visa and MasterCard no longer enjoy an exclusive relationship with banks.

In the early days, Visa and MasterCard started developing rules and standard sets of procedures for handling the flow of information so that fraud and the misuse of cards could be reduced. International processing systems were also created for both Visa and MasterCard associations, and these systems developed procedures to combat fraud as well. As credit card portfolios started to grow, issuers wanted to have more control over losses from fraud. They wanted to write rules and execute them in production soon after the transactions happened, in order to stop fraud. Also, the people in charge of the revenue and profitability figures in the banks figured out that having control of the fraud losses would help them significantly improve the profitability of the organization.

Lost-and-Stolen Fraud: The Beginnings of Fraud in Credit Cards

As credit cards were proliferating in the 1980s, consumers were using them more and more in their day-to-day lives. Most of the early fraud in credit cards was lost-and-stolen fraud. Let's say Joe Right walks into a store and forgets his card at the cash counter. A fraudster—Jack Wrong—notices that there is a credit card lying near the cashier's table. He manages to grab the card without anyone noticing. He decides to check out the card first by testing if there is any credit limit left on the card. He goes to a gas station, goes to a pump that is far away from the cashier, and charges a small amount. Once he figures out the credit card is still working (which implies that the cardholder hasn't figured out yet that he forgot his card at the store and hasn't yet reported the loss), he races to buy things that he would enjoy or things that can be easily converted to cash, such as electronics and jewelry. He needs to make these purchases quickly and in places where he is not likely to get stopped—doing a cash withdrawal at the ATM as the last stop is a good idea because there is no human interaction there. This method worked for a while, but fraudsters grew impatient because their ability to make money depended on someone forgetting their card. This led to credit card thefts where cards were stolen and used. Here too, the time the fraudsters had available to commit fraud was limited because once the cardholder figured out that his/her credit card was missing or stolen and reported it to the bank, the game was over for the fraudsters.

The fraudsters had to figure out better and more reliable ways to keep the money flowing in. The timing was right because making payments using credit cards was getting more and more impersonal. Due to the popularity of credit cards, more and more merchants accepted credit cards for payment for goods and services over the phone. If only Jack Wrong could get hold of several valid credit card numbers, he could have a field day.

Skimming of card numbers at ATM terminals and other ways of figuring out card numbers started. Skimming typically is a way to get the card numbers recorded through a hidden video camera at an ATM terminal or similar method. Once the card numbers were available, it was easy to find goods to buy and convert the goods bought to dollars. When this started happening on a massive scale, credit card issuers started demanding that merchants be held more accountable. If there was no proper verification of the cardholder's identity that was done at purchase time, the merchants should be responsible. Right? For a period of time, these fraudulent purchases were in fact the merchants' responsibility.

As merchants were setting up ways to sell their goods via the Internet, there was significant hesitation on the part of merchants to take on all of the liability. The associations had a keen interest in promoting the use of credit cards online while providing ways to protect all parties. This resulted in authentication protocols by the associations that paved a way for merchants to shift liability back to the issuers by allowing the issuers to peer into the Internet transaction as it was happening. Visa devised a verifying program at the merchants called "Verified by Visa," and MasterCard had a comparable program too which was based on the 3D Secure protocol. Once the merchants and their customers were registered in this program, merchants could shift the liability to the issuer. Interestingly, these programs— which started as a way to authenticate the cardholders during an eCommerce transaction—started to rely on behavioral models to silently authenticate a significant portion of the transactions so as not to cause abandonment of transactions midstream.

Card-Not-Present Fraud and Changes in the Marketplace

I remember participating in a panel at a conference of one of the associations back in the early 2000s. I was invited as an expert on the "security through behavior-based detection" side of the panel while the other side was "security through authentication." I remember how strongly the authentication side of the panel believed that all fraud problems could be addressed by authenticating the customer's identity. They believed that authentication is the only foolproof way. After all, in any behavior-based detection, there is always the ambiguity due to the model. Any model tells you the likelihood of a transaction being fraudulent. In theory, authentication should positively identify the customer. In theory, this seems very plausible and it seems very obvious: By requiring customers to authenticate their identity (by either entering a password or answering some security questions such as mother's maiden name, etc.), there could be big fraud savings. In reality, when customers are asked to put in a password, even legitimate cardholders may not remember it; when customers are asked intrusive questions by a website, they may not feel comfortable answering the questions. There was significant abandonment noticed in the eCommerce transactions. Hence, alongside the 3D Secure protocol, behavior-based models that allow 95 percent of the transactions without asking for passwords or answers to intrusive questions started becoming a requirement of the issuers.

While card-not-present fraud was posing significant threat in addition to lost-and-stolen fraud, there were significant changes in the marketplace. Internet merchants came into existence in the late 1990s, and using Internet sites to shop was a novelty only for a short while. Pretty soon, shopping on the Internet became the norm. Also, because of the Internet, there was another very interesting phenomenon happening. Not only could purchases be made in large quantities without ever having to interact with a human being, but the Internet could also be used to automate the entire fraud process. If Jack Wrong could get hold of the right BIN number (typically the first six digits of a credit card number—the first five digits prefixed by a zero for an American Express card and the first six digits for a Visa/MasterCard), he could generate all possible card numbers using that number. Typically, if the BIN is new, there will be a number of cards produced in the BIN with the same expiration date.

As card issuers became more sophisticated with fraud management, they started devising new methods of authentication. A card is valid only after the merchant also has the expiration date on the card (which most likely means that the user has the physical card). But using the BIN to produce all possible card numbers in the BIN is a safe strategy for the fraudster with respect to this verification. The expiration date is easy to guess with a relatively new BIN number. The verification process could be completely automated by our fraudster Jack Wrong. The strategy was to produce all possible card numbers, make a very small donation to a charitable organization, and only keep track of the cards that can be used to make the donation. Once the list of valid card numbers is known, Jack Wrong could produce the physical cards. Eventually, producing a physical card mimicking even the magnetic stripe on the card became relatively easy to do. With each level of sophistication that the issuers managed to achieve, the fraudsters could achieve even more sophistication. With physical cards in the hands of the fraudsters, major financial damage could be done.

There are some interesting issues when both the legitimate cardholder Joe Right and the fraudster Jack Wrong are transacting concurrently. Since the physical card is not missing as far as Joe Right is concerned, the length of time during which Jack Wrong could transact safely increases. Counterfeit card fraud took a strong hold and resulted in significant losses. Until Joe Right gets his statement and realizes that he didn't make some of the transactions, neither he nor his bank can be alerted to the problem.

THE ADVENT OF BEHAVIORAL MODELS

In the early 1990s, fraud was becoming a huge problem for banks. The real issue with credit card fraud was that it was unpredictable and could pretty much make or break a financial quarter for a bank. Credit cards were becoming a bigger and bigger part of a bank's assets as well as liabilities. Fraud risk was adding to credit risk (the risk of customers not paying their bills). While credit risk tends to be a much bigger chunk of overall risk dollars, fraud risk was a serious problem because it couldn't be accurately estimated. Credit risk was viewed by the banks as the cost of doing business, but fraud was considered to be something that should and could be tackled. Banks were introducing newer and newer authentication methods, but fraud was not being contained. Honestly, there was only so much banks could do in terms of authentication when the fraudster could convincingly pretend to be the real customer. This is when banks decided that it was important to look at a transaction before it got approved and not wait till the end of the day. Once you are at the end of the day, any amount of analysis that gets done is like looking in the rearview mirror. It gives you an idea of what happened without pointing to any real way of stopping fraud from happening in the future. Banks started demanding from their internal processing groups (or from an external processor if they had outsourced the processing) real-time control of the transaction using something more than just association rules.

Experts at the banks started writing rules (also known as strategies). "If the transaction amount is greater than $500, decline the transaction" could be one such rule. But the problem with this rule was that a large number of good transactions could be rejected. Every time a good transaction is declined, the banks lose valuable interchange dollars, and this affects the revenue side of the equation. Also, when a number of legitimate transactions are declined, it increases customer service calls tremendously. Excessive customer service calls are a drain on revenue as well. This is when the much-needed (but relatively simple by today's standards) nonlinear behavior-based neural network models were introduced to score the incoming transaction in the context of everything we know about the customer to decide if this particular transaction should be allowed to go through or not. These behavioral models reduced false positives, or good transactions getting declined, significantly. They were also effective at stopping fraud. The fraud losses in basis points, which had been skyrocketing, were reduced significantly by the introduction of such systems. However, there were also other factors affecting the situation.

FRAUD MANAGEMENT: AN EVOLVING CHALLENGE

While fraud itself was evolving, there were constant liability shifts between merchants and issuers in certain types of fraud. These liability shifts fundamentally changed the fraud strategies of fraud management departments. The rules followed by the association were changing as well. There was also the interesting issue of different silos in the banks not working together. For example, debit card fraud and credit card fraud are often handled quite differently. In the case of a credit card, by law, the customer is liable only for $50. Even this amount is waived most of the time. In the case of a debit card, as long as the customer reports that the card is lost, fraud losses become the bank's responsibility. So, for all practical purposes, fraud on both credit cards and debit cards has become the bank's problem: There often is no coordinated and collaborative way in which the credit and debit card fraud management departments operate.

"Bust-out" fraud causes another interesting quandary in any bank. Suppose Jack Wrong decides to file a fraudulent application, manages to secure a card, and starts charging on the card with the clear intent to pay the bill for a month or so, charge up and leave. What do we conclude in terms of the dollar loss? Sometimes this is classified as credit risk as opposed to fraud. One of the reasons that this classification into the fraud or the credit risk buckets becomes difficult to do is because the dollar amounts tend to be large, and both credit risk and fraud departments have a vested interest in classifying this loss in the other department's accounting. If this is fraud and gets classified as credit risk, the information is totally lost to the fraud models. One portion of the fraud that should be made available to the model or rule to learn from simply ceases to exist. Breaking down some of the silos and being able to measure all of these different types of risk side by side is going to be essential to solving this problem in the future. This can only be achieved by a true enterprise system. It is important not to get bogged down in the process of determining whose loss it is. If all the systems talk to each other, and any loss from fraud can be addressed effectively, *where* the loss should be counted from an accounting perspective becomes less important. Some of the most recent technological advancements make this possible.

Fraud management is justifiably considered a Sisyphean task, but it is significantly different from the task Sisyphus faced. Unlike the monotonous task of rolling the boulder up, fraud management is a constantly changing and an evolving challenge. One can never rest on one's laurels when it comes to fraud management. Change and continual improvement are the only constant features of this quest to control fraud. For the same reason, it is important not to let the fraud management system stagnate and not to use technology that is over a decade old. The fraud management system also needs to be changing and adapting to the nature of fraud by using the most sophisticated techniques available. Some of the changes needed are putting better systems in place; some of the changes focus on using the data better and investing in better techniques; some of the changes are around operationalizing the detection systems better.

From a systems perspective, being able to make the transaction data available to fraud detection in a very timely fashion is extremely important. If there is no way to provide the data in real time to the system that is making the decision, even the most sophisticated fraud detection system will not be effective. Once the money flows out of the door, the attempt to contain fraud will lose effectiveness. When the data is made available to the fraud detection system, the system should be able to decide on the transaction very quickly and return a recommendation of what needs to be done with that particular transaction. To reach a decision, the system needs to take into consideration the context of what we are used to observing as normal for this cardholder as well as some important entities associated with this cardholder.

For example, if you look at the current challenges in fraud management, it is not enough to simply observe a cardholder's past behavior and evaluate whether this transaction resembles the cardholder's typical behavior. It is also important to observe the behavior of multiple entities involved in the transaction. If both husband and wife are charging on their card at a risky foreign location, it is less indicative of fraud (most likely the pair is traveling abroad) than if only one of them is charging at the location (likely that one card is compromised). There is no way to figure out this information unless we are observing the account entity that has the cards issued under the account (for example, two cards for each spouse issued under a single account). Similarly, there is no way we can identify fraud occurring at an ATM terminal where there is exactly one transaction on each compromised card unless we can observe what is normal for the ATM terminal and what is not. So, even though it may be the first $100 withdrawal on Joe Right's card, we can figure out fraud has occurred because there have been twenty $100 withdrawals at this terminal, each on a distinct card. Multi-entity behavioral modeling that is based on sophisticated nonlinear modeling techniques is a requirement for addressing this problem effectively. These are some of the latest advancements in the area of fraud detection.

FRAUD DETECTION ACROSS DOMAINS

Looking at multiple entities simultaneously to more precisely detect fraud is needed for other domains and products as well. Let's consider another example. In order to understand if a particular batch of ACH transactions has a fraudulent transaction embedded in it, it will be important to understand the multiple entities involved in the batch— for example, the originator (the entity initiating the transaction), the beneficiary (the entity receiving the amount), and the analyst (the accounting analyst initiating the transaction on behalf of the originator). A transaction may be totally normal for an originator but may be totally out of the ordinary for the originator–beneficiary combination. Let's say that a mom & pop grocery store is used to making payments of $1,000 to $1,500 to various vendors, but this originator making a payment to the beneficiary "Rent-a-Wreck" is not normal. If only the originators and the associated amounts are studied, this anomaly will not be detected as there are many amounts in this range that the originator routinely disburses. However, if the combination of originator and beneficiary and the nature of the beneficiary are considered, it will become clear very quickly that there is a strong possibility of fraud. Considering multiple entities and studying their behaviors is extremely important to accurately detect fraud in a number of domains.

These examples do not have to be limited to the financial industry. Whether it is network intrusion detection or identifying anomalous activity at an Internet site or figuring out abnormal purchase behavior or whatever, there is no absolute definition of "normal" and "abnormal" we can use to classify activity into different buckets. What is normal for one entity may be totally abnormal for another entity. Without context, no model can make sense of what is going on. The context needs to be provided in as many ways as possible without sacrificing speed. It is also important to find the efficient frontier and stop there. What is normal for an entity A with respect to one entity X may not be normal for the same entity A with respect to another entity Y. These combinations and the entities themselves have to be studied and considered in the context of the activity and the phenomenon that we are detecting to truly understand what is going on. The use of such science is only beginning in multiple industries, and that is what will make data science so exciting in the future.

Interpreting data multidimensionally and understanding what is normal and what is not is important requires multiple techniques. Different techniques have different levels of efficacy in these assessments. If the same data is provided to a simple model versus a complex model, depending on whether the underlying phenomenon can be explained simply or requires some complex interpretations, using simple techniques will cause the efficacy of the models to suffer. The evolution of various analytic techniques to detect risk is discussed in detail in Chapter Seven ("Fraud Analytics: We Are Just Scratching the Surface"). Fraud detection techniques have come a long way, but the best is yet to come. The important idea to keep in mind is to make sure the fraud management departments are using the most sophisticated and operationally practical and usable fraud detection system on the market. The operational usability of the system is very important. If a very sophisticated model cannot be run fast enough in real time to return a decision in several milliseconds in production, the sophistication of the model doesn't mean much in terms of containing losses. Investing in sophistication and following a practical, usable approach are both very important. The most sophisticated models are just theoretical exercises if they cannot be used in real time 100 percent of the time.

USING FRAUD DETECTION EFFECTIVELY

Even after we have implemented a fraud detection system that is based on sophisticated techniques and that can execute effectively in real time, it is important for the operational staff to use the recommendations of the system effectively. There are three ways that fraud management can improve results with even a highly sophisticated system.

The first (and very common) strategy is never to allow operational staff to second-guess a sophisticated model. Very often, a model score of 900 (let's say this is an indicator of very high fraud risk), when combined with some decision keys and sometimes on its own, can perform extremely well. It would be a good idea to use the scores at this risky range as is and not allow the analysts to add further nuances to it. This will have to be completely understood and controlled at the operational level. Using a well-developed fraud score as is without watering it down is one of the most important operational strategies.

Second, fraud analysts will have to be trained to use the scores and the reason codes (reason codes explain why the score is indicative of risk) effectively in operations. Typically, this is done by writing some rules in operations that incorporate the scores and reason codes as decision keys. In the fraud management world, these rules are generally referred to as strategies. It is extremely important to ensure strategies are applied uniformly by all fraud analysts. It is essential to closely monitor how the fraud analysts are operating using the scores and strategies.

Third, it is very important to train the analysts to mark transactions that are confirmed or reported to be fraudulent by the customers accurately in their data store.

All three of these strategies may seem very simple to accomplish, but in practical terms, they are not that easy without a lot of planning, time, and energy. A superior fraud detection system can be rendered almost useless if it is not used correctly. It is extremely important to allow the right level of employee to exercise the right level of judgment. A fraud analyst should not be allowed to second-guess the efficacy of a fraud score that is the result of a sophisticated model. Similarly, planners of operations should take into account all practical limitations while coming up with fraud strategies. Ensuring that all of this gets done the right way with the right emphasis ultimately leads to good, effective fraud management.

At the heart of any fraud detection system is a rule or a model that attempts to detect a behavior that has been observed repeatedly in various frequencies in the past and classifies it as fraud or non-fraud with a certain rank ordering. We would like to figure out this behavior in advance and stop it in its tracks. What we observe from historical data and our experience needs be converted to some sort of a rule that can be systematically applied to the data in the future. We expect that these rules or models will improve our chance of detecting aberrations in behavior and help us distinguish between genuine customers and fraudsters in a timely manner. The goal is to stop the bleeding of cash from the account and accomplish that as close to the start of the fraud episode as we can. If banks can accurately identify early indicators of fraud, significant losses can be avoided.

In statistical terms, what we define as fraud would be the dependent variable or the variable we are trying to predict (or detect) using a model. We would try to use a few independent variables or *so-called* independent variables (as many of the variables used in the model tend to have some dependency on each other in real life) to detect fraud. Fundamentally, we are trying to model the fraud problem using these independent variables. Typically, a model attempts to *detect* fraud as opposed to *predict* fraud. We are not trying to say that fraud is likely to happen on this entity in the future; rather, we are trying to determine whether fraud is likely happening at the present moment, and the goal of the fraud model is to identify this as close to the time that the fraud started as possible. In credit risk management, we try to predict if there will likely be serious delinquency or default risk in the future, based on the behavior exhibited in the entity today.

With respect to detecting fraud, during the model-building process, not having accurate fraud data is akin to not knowing what the target is in a shooting range. If a model or rule is built on data that is only 75 percent accurate, it is going to cause the model's accuracy and effectiveness to be suspect as well. There are two sides to this problem.

Suppose we mark 25 percent of the fraudulent transactions inaccurately as non-fraud or good transactions. Not only are we missing out on learning from a significant portion of fraudulent behavior, by misclassifying it as non-fraud, it leads to the model assuming the behavior is actually good behavior. Hence, misclassification of data affects both sides of the equation. Accurate fraud data is fundamental to addressing the fraud problem effectively.

Collecting accurate fraud data is not the responsibility of just one set of people in the bank. The entire mind-set of the organization should be geared around collecting, preserving, and using the data effectively. We will look at the importance of participation from the entire organization to accomplish this goal in Chapter Six ("The Chain Is Only as Strong as Its Weakest Link").

Interestingly, the fraud data challenges faced by a number of other industries are very similar. Banks are probably further along in fraud management and can provide a number of pointers to other industries, but fundamentally, the problem is the same everywhere. Hence, a number of techniques detailed in this book are applicable to a number of industries, even though most of the examples used in the book are based on banks. In the near future, we will no doubt witness the impact of effective risk management in multiple industries.

SUMMARY

The history of credit and debit cards has approximately tracked the growth in sophistication in data-driven risk management. I studied statistics at a time when it was fashionable to criticize it. It is very satisfying now to see the widespread use of statistical models to address several day-to-day problems. The important thing to remember is what Professor George E. P. Box said: "All models are wrong; some are useful."[7] He went on to say, "We have a large reservoir of engineers (and scientists) with a vast background of engineering know-how. They need to learn statistical methods that can tap into the knowledge. Statistics used as a catalyst to engineering creation will, I believe, always result in the fastest and most economical progress. . . . "[8] This is equally important whether one is trying to be a power user of an environment powered by models or is simply preparing the environment to provide the data needed for the model.

While data-driven methods certainly have an element of rocket science to them, many of the fundamental steps to build and use sophisticated data-driven risk management systems are basic steps that any good IT department can effectively take. We will be examining the essential ingredients of the process in more detail in the coming chapters.

CHAPTER 3

In God We Trust. The Rest Bring Data!

herlock Holmes (in the short story "The Adventures of the Copper Beeches" by Sir Arthur Conan Doyle) summarizes nicely what I want to say about the importance of data: "Data! Data! Data! I can't make bricks without clay!"[1]

I am sure anyone with a serious interest in the area of data-driven predictive modeling has heard that a strong positive correlation between two variables does not imply a causal relationship. Very often, this is as used as an argument against statistical modeling. It is a widely held opinion that domain expertise is much more important than what the data shows. This argument certainly has some merit. Just because there is relationship between two quantities, we cannot conclude that one is the cause of the other.

Here is an example that I have occasionally used to prove the validity of this statement: If we look at the correlation between the monetary damage caused by fires in a certain city and the number of fire engines sent to the scene of the fire, there is likely to be a significant correlation. In other words, the sites with higher monetary damage would probably have had a higher number of fire engines working to contain the fire as well. A naïve modeler could build a model to predict the monetary damage caused by a fire (the dependent variable) that uses the number of fire engines as an independent variable. Based on this, are we right to conclude that next time there is a fire, we can reduce the monetary damage by sending fewer fire engines to the fire site? No. That would lead to the exact opposite result. While there is a strong correlation between the two quantities, the increase in the number of fire engines is not what causes the increases in monetary damage. If the damage is higher, the size and complexity of the fire episode is higher, and this can likely be contained only by sending more fire trucks. If we want to convert this correlation to a causal relationship, it is important that such a relationship actually seems plausible. In this case, it is clearly not plausible.

This side of the argument—the argument that we should try to make sense of the model using domain expertise—has been used often. However, it is not enough to look at only one side of this equation. While this side of the equation has been examined many times, in this age of data proliferation and increasingly complex phenomena that are less and less understood by even domain experts, it is equally important to examine the other side of the equation—namely, without adequate data, can we conclude that a causal relationship exists between two phenomena, especially in behavioral modeling? I have seen more errors of this latter kind than the former. I should rush to say that the bias is clearly due to the line of work I have engaged in. In this chapter, we will go through the ten guidelines to be followed to set up the right data environment so that adequate data can be used to draw sound conclusions on business issues.

DATA ANALYSIS AND CAUSAL RELATIONSHIPS

Sir Arthur Conan Doyle, physician and famous writer, once said, "It is a capital mistake to theorize before one has data."[2] An even more convincing statement comes from General Colin Powell, who says "Experts often possess more data than judgment."[3] True experts look at data carefully and question everything for which there is not enough evidence. While there is a lot of literature on how it is a mistake to depend on data to establish causal relationships, history is filled with instances of believing in a theory without proof for far too long. In my observation, there has been more erring on the side of trusting judgment too much rather than depending on data too much. A number of times, when the data shows something different from what we believe to be the truth, observing the phenomenon closer and collecting more data will tell us more about the data as well as the phenomenon. An added complication in using data to draw conclusions is the scarcity of true data analysis and good interpretation experts. The demand for people who can make sense of data has been on a dramatic rise over the last two decades, and I don't see that abating anytime soon.

There are several examples of the importance of using data to ascertain a theory before assuming it is true. For the longest time, it was believed that the earth was at the center of the universe. As early as the third century B.C., Greek astronomer and mathematician Aristarchus of Samos[4] offered theories opposing this and proposing the sun as the center, but they were largely ignored. For centuries the theory that the earth was at the center of the universe was believed to be true, with no real data supporting the theory. From the second century to the sixteenth century, Ptolemy's theory that the earth was at the center of the universe was accepted until the sixteenth century when Tycho Brahe (whose theory had some faults but was a huge improvement over the pure geocentric theory) and Copernicus[5] proved that the earth was orbiting around the sun, using data they had collected. This was a clear case of theory being proved wrong by data.

Here is another example. Until the Michelson and Morley experiment was conducted in the late nineteenth century,[6] it was widely believed that ether was needed for electromagnetic wave transmission. Data proved that the ether theory was wrong. Another example: The continental drift theory[7] was not accepted for hundreds of years, until a lot of data was collected and presented. There have been numerous cases where a theory that is held to be true is completely proved wrong by data. There have also been numerous cases where a theory that is held to be wrong is completely proved correct by data. In experimental physics, there are a number of theories that get established and nuanced by successive data collection exercises. While data collection is essential to establishing the correctness of a number of facts, critics of statistical analysis have tended to focus on how data can be used incorrectly to establish causal relationships when there are none.

Let's say we believe in a causal relationship between two quantities. If there is no data to support the assumption that the relationship exists, are we right in endorsing the causal relationship, assuming it is possible to collect data on the relationship? For the purpose of this illustration, I would like to limit this argument to just behavioral phenomena that can be proved loosely at best. I am not referring to well-known scientific facts. In the realm of behavioral modeling, while correlations may or may not imply causal relationships, causal relationships not reflected in the data collected cannot confirm these relationships either. This is a concept that doesn't get discussed as often but one that is very important in order to understand behavioral modeling. If the data doesn't support the theory, collecting more data is a good idea, but most likely the theory is flawed as well. Collecting data is not possible in all realms of science, but wherever possible, data holds the key to a lot of very important secrets. Sometimes even in areas where collecting data is easy, not enough attention gets paid to data collection. There are a number of areas of research where conclusions are drawn about phenomena without enough data.

BEHAVIORAL MODELING IN FINANCIAL INSTITUTIONS

In my previous life as a biostatistician where my work involved applying statistics to a wide range of topics in biology with special emphasis on applications to medicine, one of the most challenging parts of my job was being forced to draw conclusions based on experiments that had very few—sometimes as few as a dozen—subjects. Once I was helping a medical researcher set up a study and he was insisting on having 13 rats as subjects in a study of a new version of an orthopedic surgical procedure. I tried to convince him that we needed to include many more rats in the study in order to draw any meaningful conclusions from the data. He insisted on having 13 subjects, so I asked him why, and his answer was "The previous researcher in this area used

12 subjects and I want to use one more." This caused me to almost fall off my chair.

While directionally it is a good goal to have more subjects in the study than the previous researcher, conclusions drawn on the surgical method using only 13 subjects are very unlikely to be valid. Also, any good research based on data needs to have some solid understanding of the minimum sample sizes needed. There are a number of areas of science where for a number of reasons it is simply impossible to get enough subjects for a study. However, this is not the case with all research studies. One of my pet peeves is that even in areas where it is possible to get more subjects (in the above example, it would have been very easy to use 40 or so rats as subjects), not enough attention is paid to having enough data. This in turn causes the concept of statistics to get some notoriety. Such studies are unlikely to yield results that would stand the test of time. However, it is the poorly designed study's fault—statistics itself is not to blame!

When we talk about modeling for risk management in financial institutions, the good news is that there is no scarcity of data. The central limit theorem (CLT) may have limitations because of other reasons but not because of sample size in the risk management arena. The level of data available in banks and the lack of personal behavioral information available on customers allow for behavioral modeling to flourish in various areas of customer management in banks, not just risk management. Behavioral models are slowly becoming the mainstay in customer treatment decisions in banks. I believe this is an extremely positive trend and one that opens up a number of excellent possibilities.

So, what is behavioral modeling, and why is it important? Today, banks and other institutions are facing the following dilemma: The customer base they have is much larger than before, the data they have collected on these customers is huge and increasing by the day, the relationships they have with the customers are much less personal than before, and the amount of time they have to react to the next request from the customer is measured in split seconds. Along with all this, the expectation of customers today is that the institution has a thorough understanding of who they are and that the institution should be able to read their minds and figure out exactly what the customers are looking for. Despite no real personal knowledge of customers, the banks are expected to have a grasp of their desires to be able to react appropriately to each customer during every interaction. The level of expectation from sophisticated and unsophisticated customers alike is very high.

Customer Expectations versus Standards of Privacy

I have been consistently baffled by an interesting dichotomy that exists today in the realm of customer expectations. Most customers get annoyed by the level of personal information about them that gets gleaned by various organizations in every interaction they have. This kind of customer annoyance was almost unheard of a few decades ago. Imagine this: If a banker in the 1970s had greeted a customer trying to withdraw $20 in cash with "Hello, Mr. Smith, I remember that you preferred your cash withdrawal in $5 bills last time, so here is the $20 you withdrew in $5 bills," I am sure Mr. Smith would have been very pleased with the bank. It was a way for the bank to improve the relationship with the customer. Mr. Smith would have actually felt safe with the bank because he would have felt that someone has personal knowledge of his account as well as his personal likes and dislikes and hence will take care of his needs.

Today, let's say I am surfing on the Internet and an ad pops up: "Would you like to visit a craft store? Here is a coupon for $5 to use at Michaels," my reaction is somewhat different from that of Mr. Smith's a few decades ago. I feel a bit happy about my $5 coupon, but then the feeling changes to mild annoyance and circumspection due to the perceived invasion of my privacy ("How does this site know I am crazy about crafts? Am I giving away too much information about myself on the Internet? I have to be more careful with what I do on the Internet"). The thought that then follows is totally different. "Don't they know I like beads better? How come they don't have a coupon for a specialist bead store instead of Michaels? Shouldn't they know that I don't visit Michaels often these days?"

I have caught myself thinking how unsophisticated an institution is if it pops the same ad in front of me every time I log on to its site. For a long time, I thought that my specific series of thoughts were biased by my decades-long experience as a data scientist. However, what I find in a number of interactions with my friends and family is that even non–data scientists have similar expectations of the institutions they do business with. I am not unique in terms of my expectations. Customer expectations have gone up tremendously in the last couple of decades. Having said that, it is important to analyze and understand the irony of the situation—the customer on one hand expects the institution to know more about him/her so that he/she can be treated right, but then doesn't feel great about his/her personal likes and dislikes being known to so many organizations. In essence, customer expectations are totally different now compared to a few decades ago, and a lot of these expectations are guided by what technology has gotten us accustomed to. Customers expect a lot in terms of how they should be treated in a particular transaction, while at the same time they have high standards regarding how their privacy needs should be protected.

What is behavioral modeling? It is the technique we use to observe the behavior of a customer through his/her transactions and use our observations to accurately predict future behavior of the customer; it is also used to detect if the current transaction is likely a transaction initiated by the customer or possibly initiated by a fraudster as the pattern doesn't fit the predicted expectations from this customer.

How exactly is a behavioral model built? The data associated with the transactions is used to create various features accurately representing the underlying behavior of the entity. These features are used in statistical models, such as linear or logistic regression, neural networks, and so on. The output of the model can be interpreted as the probability of associated risk. This probability gets converted to a score used to rank order risk. The goal of behavioral modeling is to provide a good rank ordering among customers to decide if taking a specific action would add value. The better the rank ordering, the better the end results will be.

When making fraud-related decisions, the idea is to impact as few non-fraud customers and their transactions as possible. When making marketing-related decisions, the goal is to improve the response rate or the revenue on a campaign as much as possible while avoiding sending any marketing offers to customers the bank shouldn't be marketing to.

Behavioral modeling done right can yield great results and increase profits; badly executed behavioral modeling, though, could cause the opposite effect and pretty much ruin the financials of the institution. In problems like fraud management where split-second results are the norm, modeling not done right can be very detrimental.

The Importance of Data in Implementing Good Behavioral Models

Behavioral modeling is no longer a luxury. It has become a necessity in the realm of risk management as well as customer service. The day when data and superior models are the real differentiators for any organization is not far off. If we look at today's behavioral models, the level of sophistication can vary widely. Some are very simple heuristic models; some are simple rules; some are complex rules; some are linear statistical models; some are sophisticated nonlinear models; some are very sophisticated nonlinear multi-entity based models. I have listed these roughly in ascending order of sophistication and effectiveness. Typically, the more complex the models, the better the results. I will go over some of the levels of sophistication and the results achieved at each level in detail in Chapter Seven ("Fraud Analytics: We Are Just Scratching the Surface"). In that chapter, I will use a simple simulated dataset to illustrate the effect of increasing levels of model sophistication.

In this chapter, I discuss specifically the importance of data in implementing good behavioral models, regardless of the level of sophistication used in building the model. Whether we use a set of bricks to build a small wall or a small house or a big house or a mansion or an architectural wonder like the Taj Mahal, the strength of the building and how long it will last is determined by the quality of the bricks we use. In order for the structure to survive over a long period of time, it is important to build the structure with high-quality ingredients. One of the most crucial ingredients in behavioral modeling is the data we collect over the period of time that includes the phenomena we are interested in predicting or detecting. Using this data, we draw conclusions on what to do when a phenomenon (fraud, credit risk, or anything we tried to stop in the past and couldn't) happens again in the future. The process of figuring out how certain transactions were conducted during the period of interest sheds light on the risk. This generally begins with collecting and assembling the data.

SETTING UP A DATA ENVIRONMENT

The title of this chapter is "In God We Trust. The Rest Bring Data!" This is literally the mantra that needs to be followed in any data-driven problem. We hope also that the data that is collected is in good shape in terms of quality and definitions. Setting up any good data environment requires a cultural and organizational shift in the organization so that the entire organization understands the strategic importance of data. At a tactical level, this process involves certain important guidelines to be followed. While these ten guidelines are stated with banks in mind, they could apply to any organization with interest in data to solve difficult, valuable, hard-to-solve problems. Here are the ten guidelines:

1. Know your data.
2. Collect all the data you can from day one.
3. Allow for additions as the data grows.
4. If you cannot integrate the data, you cannot integrate the businesses.
5. When you want to change the definition of a field, it is best to augment, not modify.
6. Document the data you have as well as the data you lost.
7. When change happens, document it.
8. ETL: "Extract, Translate, Load" (not "Extract, Taint, Lose").
9. A data model is an impressionist painting.
10. The top two assets of any business today are people and data.

1. Know Your Data

In the course of my career over the last two decades, I have been involved in many data exercises in many different capacities across multiple industries solving problems ranging all the way from risk management to marketing to network intrusion to tax underfiling.

It is always fascinating to watch the number of iterations of inter-pretations of the data fields the teams have to go through before a clear picture of what is being sought emerges. The other noticeable commonality is also that, whether the organization believes in too much documenting or doesn't document enough, there are always a few key individuals in the organization who have the knowledge of these fields in their heads, and this knowledge is typically limited to just a few individuals. I have found this to be almost uniformly true. The amount of effort that is put into the understanding and upkeep of systems is usually far greater than the effort that gets in-vested in the data assets at the institution. I believe that, in the next few decades, the institutions that excel at handling the data side of the assets are going to have a tremendous edge over institutions that don't. Knowledge of data should be much more widespread than a few individuals who happen to be involved in accumulating and assembling the data.

The data assets of the organizations need to guarded carefully. The extensive documenting and searching facilities that computers make possible today should be fully exploited. Also, educating the entire organization on both good and bad examples of how having good data or not having good data respectively can improve or affect downstream processes can help put things in context for the entire organization. This often requires a cultural change in the organization.

The key points here are that it is important for organizations to know the data that is available and to make this knowledge wide-spread within the organization so that it is not known to just a few people. This is extremely important now and about to become even more important in the near future.

2. Collect All the Data You Can from Day One

If you ask any modeler how much data they would like to get on a project, the first answer you will usually hear is "the more data the better." There are of course practical limitations to what can be used for a project due to a number of considerations, such as whether the data would be applicable to the current problem, whether extrapola-tions using the data would actually make sense, whether the data is available in operations so that a model using this data can be used in production to streamline operations, and so on. However, with data storage as inexpensive as it is now, it is to an organization's clear advantage to collect and store as much data as practically possible.

Periodic aligning the amount of data stored to the current cost of data storage will be an extremely fruitful exercise. Many a time I have felt that there is no internal consistency between the real cost of storage and the decisions made by IT to store only a certain number of months of data. Data storage decisions in older institutions tend not to keep pace with the dropping cost of storage. Today, it seems that there is nothing to lose in terms of cost. From day one of setting up a data environment, it is very important to make allowances for collecting all the data and collecting it in as detailed a fashion as possible.

For example, if there are ten different codes used to quantify a particular field, it always makes sense to capture them as granularly as possible instead of collapsing categories and losing information in the process. If one particular project does not need a lot of categories, it would be straightforward to collapse some of the 10 categories into a single category to ensure that all the raw material is available when needed. It doesn't make sense to lose all this information while starting to collect the data and deciding on the data definitions. Too often some key fields become less useful because the information is not granular enough. This is especially true in environments where the data storage is in databases. A lot of information gets condensed beyond recognition and becomes a lot less useful than it could be. Quite often, the process of metadata layer development for databases doesn't involve the modeling experts who can ensure that data integrity and granularity are preserved. There is generally a misguided tendency to involve modelers only at the last stage of information extraction, namely model building. Modeler involvement should start at the beginning, right from the time data is extracted and assembled. This often results in a major cultural shift of viewing data as a tremendous asset within the organization.

Related to this, I have watched with great interest the development of data science as a key field of the future. To me, the key differentiator between the traditional environment and the emerging data environments fueled by data science is the following: An environment that is driven by data science integrates the understanding of the data with predictive modeling and the deployment of the models in the production environment very tightly and does not look at data management/preparation, modeling, and deployment as three separate functions that don't have to interrelate.

I was lucky to start my career in a data-driven environment and help grow such environments over the last two decades. It is very interesting and gratifying to see this idea gaining universal acceptance. The key to excellence in data-driven decisions is developing an environment that values and understands the importance of data. Next are some examples of why this is important.

To draw an example from the world of card authorizations, a number of fraud strategies rely on knowing whether a particular authorization (usually resulting from some form of purchase) is due to a card-present or card-not-present transaction. Whether a transaction was conducted in a card-present or card-not-present manner is certainly good information to have and delineates fraud risk. However, to have data one more level of detail below each one of these categories is much more useful, especially in international portfolios. Under the card-not-present category, knowing whether the transaction was keyed or eCommerce is very useful. Under the card-present category, knowing whether the transaction was swiped, or swiped with magnetic stripe, or chip (whether it was made at a chip-enabled terminal and forced to fall back to swipe) all help determine the likelihood of fraud much better than if we only had the two top-level categories. It is important to preserve all the different combinations underneath the top-level categories.

Having granular data from day one can be a huge differentiator. It is also important to have regular backups of the data and have all of the past data available in storage as the data grows. This is especially important in environments where data can be stored online only for a certain time period.

Periodic quality checks of the data need to be done to ensure that the data is being recorded per the original definitions. Often data environments start off with a set of clean definitions but veer off in different directions, and sometimes data that is not used for some specific goal can lose quality. This is an important consideration to value. While data environments are getting set up, the process(es) of checking the data periodically also needs to be set up.

The key points in this category are that with respect to data, more is always better and keeping past data easily accessible gives the financial institution more options. Also, individual definitions need to be as granular as possible (within practical constraints, of course). Regular backups of data and monitoring the online data as well as backed-up data are both very important.

3. Allow for Additions as the Data Grows

The number of fields as well as the amount of data collected will always be on the increase. Whatever data is available on certain transactions, it is important for banks to capture this information in a timely fashion and make the data available for downstream processes. While I understand that banking systems can be very complex and changes are hard to make, all too often I have noticed that important pieces of information are made available by the associations in the transactions but the banks take a long time to capture the information and make the additional data part of their regular data streams. Visa and MasterCard associations usually add fields after a lot of research, and the added fields are typically very valuable. Losing the first several months of this data could mean losing competitive advantage. The ability of the system to be flexible enough to allow for timely additions in data helps to capture rich information as quickly as possible. Having the data available earlier than other banks would be an excellent competitive edge. Fundamentally, if the systems are built to allow additions in the future, it will be far easier to capture additional pieces of information in a timely manner. Some simple measures like allowing for a buffer of easily accessible space at the end of the transactions, allocating people to look at data changes on a regular basis to integrate with the existing data streams, and building data integration tools that can make this process easier instead of reinventing the process every single time are some ways in which data additions can be addressed. Smoothing out this process is a good idea for any organization that uses data to solve key business problems.

Many a business problem can be solved effectively by laying down some or all of these processes at the very beginning of setting up the data environment. The introduction of columnar databases in big data environments is a great advancement in the area of database storage. The days of waiting several weeks to a few months to add a few fields to a database should be a thing of the past. This will be a *need* for future data environments, not a *want*.

The key points under this guideline are that a good system of capturing data should be able to react to changes/additions quickly and to capture the information as quickly as possible after the changes take effect. Having information available in a timely fashion is a key competitive advantage.

4. If You Cannot Integrate the Data, You Cannot Integrate the Businesses

One of the biggest challenges banks face today is consolidation in the financial marketplace and how often business units are bought and sold by banks. The data from two organizations—even when they are in the same business—can look radically different in terms of content, granularity in classification, and quality. While a lot of time and energy is spent on integrating the companies from a people-and-process perspective, typically there is little attention paid to integrating the data assets of the two companies. It is well known in the industry that even years after an acquisition or merger is completed, the data assets of the two companies are maintained separately and hence action on the customers may have to be taken differently between the two entities. There is also no true integration of the data to enable understanding the customer base as a whole. There is significant loss of opportunity when months and months pass without the data coming together. It is extremely important to integrate the data into the same format and meaning before the integration of the companies is considered to be complete.

Really, businesses cannot be integrated until their data assets are integrated, brought under one umbrella, and understood. If this is not done, the original intent of growing the business suffers. Interestingly, this is an area that gets overlooked very regularly in business integration. A plan for integrating the data assets of two merging companies should be done at the time of the merger. This plan needs to be put into action swiftly. The integration of the two entities should not be considered complete until their data assets have been integrated completely so that action can be taken on customers as if the two merged entities are a single business. This seems like a simple idea but it gets routinely overlooked in many acquisitions.

The key points to remember under this guideline are that in an acquisition or merger, integration of data should be planned and accounted for as a key step in the overall integration plan. The businesses won't truly come together until the data comes together.

5. When You Want to Change the Definition of a Field, It Is Best to Augment and Not Modify

It is typical for a data field to start with a certain definition or a set of codes, and as the information captured in the data field becomes more important operationally, the data field definition tends to get augmented. Too often, the augmented definition tends to override code that was used for a certain purpose and tries to use the same code for a different purpose. Unless the change is done after meticulously taking into account all of the impacts, the data collected in the fields before the change happened tends to become useless after the change.

A classic example of this type of problem is the difference between time-on-books and time-since-first-transaction. These two fields are completely different in meaning and the values they carry. An account that has been on the books for six months but started transacting only last week would have completely different values for this field if we decide to replace time-on-books with time-since-first-transaction. Such issues and data problems can easily be avoided if there is a uniform policy that any change or addition to a field should only augment it and not change its essential meaning. Say two fields need to be brought together. It is a good idea to evaluate if it is really necessary, or if an additional field should be introduced so that both pieces of information are captured in both systems. Sometimes problems can be addressed very effectively by adding fields rather than modifying the meaning of fields. A little bit of careful thought helps a lot in this area.

The key point of this topic is to make sure all field definition changes are done as additions to existing codes and not replacements of existing codes. Banks should strive to create an environment where the data is sacrosanct. This environment has to be created and fostered very carefully so that the entire organization thinks along the same lines.

6. Document the Data You Have as Well as the Data You Lost

In any large data-processing environment, unfortunately, it is inevitable that sometimes data fails to get saved. Often it is impossible to re-create this data. The data that is lost could be just a chunk of transactions during the day. It could be an entire transmission of files. It could be several hours or even days' worth of data. Almost always, the knowledge of this missing data resides in the heads of a few key personnel, and information on the missing data almost never gets recorded. Months later, when the historical data is extracted and assembled for a modeling or other project, countless cycles are spent on detective work to figure out why the frequencies are fluctuating during certain days. The information that the data was simply missed on these days is not available immediately. After going through a few iterations of questions and going round and round and talking to different data experts, just when finding the source of these fluctuations starts to be a wild goose chase, sudden knowledge emerges that there was actually missing data on the days in question. A lot of this work could be avoided if the habit of documenting known missing data is encouraged and becomes part of the normal process. This seems like a simple step but it is almost never done, and the cycles spent on finding this information could be better spent on other tasks.

The key point in this section is to remember that documenting missing data is every bit as important as general documentation of data that is available. Once it is ascertained that pieces of data are missing, it is important to document the information and make it widely available. This will avoid cycles being wasted on chasing information on lost data. This documentation should be readily accessible and available whenever data is being assembled for a project.

7. When Change Happens, Document It

Obviously, changes must be documented. However, it is surprising how many times changes are *not* documented. I have noticed that most changes in data are usually unearthed not because of the documentation provided by the banks but because of the in-depth data analysis that happens in every project. The data analysis process throws up anomalies observed in the data, which, on repeated examination, results in raising a spark in a data expert's brain cells. It is somewhat disconcerting to see how many of these changes are documented only in the memory of some key personnel. I personally am not a big fan of too much documentation, and I think what Winston Churchill said about lengthy documents is absolutely right and applies to any lengthy documentation as well. He said famously, "The length of this document defends it well against the risk of it being read."[8] Every time I think of this quote, I marvel at its wisdom. While more might not be good with respect to documentation, there is a minimum requirement for crisp documentation to keep track of crucial changes in data. This documentation needs to be done to protect against large quantities of data being rendered useless in future data exercises. Too often, information about data changes is lost forever because it doesn't get recorded anywhere. As data-driven techniques that illuminate the nuances of various changes in data become used more widely, it is crucial to differentiate missing data from drops in data.

The key point here is that a well-thought-through, crisp, to-the-point documentation of changes is key to the smooth functioning of the data environment and protection against large quantities of data being unusable in future data exercises.

8. ETL: "Extract, Translate, Load" (Not "Extract, Taint, Lose")

With the proliferation of very large data warehouses, there is a real need to move data from one location to another—typically from large production files to large data warehouses. ETL (Extract, Translate, Load) processes are well defined to handle the data volumes smoothly while adhering to the overall processes already established. These processes understand the data models of the warehouses very well and do a fairly good job of translating the data from the original location to the new data warehouse(s). What we find very often, though, is that the granularity of the data, which directly contributes to the data's richness, is often compromised because of the ETL processes. The ETL process can attempt to translate too much of the information, consolidating the data under broad categories instead of preserving the granularity in the underlying data. Instead of the process simply moving the data from one location to the other, the process tends to taint and lose a significant amount of the information while executing. For example, let's say there are 30 different customer categories in the production data and they are named serially from 1 to 30. If the ETL attempts to process this into 10 categories and it also only allows numbers in a certain range (say 1 to 12), the mapping of the 30 categories has to be done carefully so that a minimum of data is lost. Also, because of the restriction in the range, we will have to make sure that there is enough room for future growth in the categories. Defining these ETL processes is an art and a science. Very often, they are not artfully defined, and that causes a lot of information to get lost.

The key takeaway from this guideline is to make sure that ETL processes are defined thoughtfully to preserve the granularity in the underlying data. The ETL processes should be defined to transport the data to a different environment while maintaining the data's integrity. ETL processes should not be used to redefine data captured in a different environment. The aim is to make sure that the data doesn't get tainted and lost in translation.

9. A Data Model Is an Impressionist Painting

Whenever I think of a good data model (not referring to behavioral models here) defined to bring together data from multiple sources, I am reminded of an impressionist painting. I have always had a very deep admiration for impressionist paintings, not just for their beauty while you look at them from afar, but also due to how amazingly well the seemingly unconnected small painting strokes are assembled carefully to create a masterpiece. When the individual strokes are looked at, it would be hard to visualize the role of one particular stroke in the overall picture. When you look at the picture from a distance, then you look closely at an individual stroke, it becomes obvious how important that small stroke was in bringing the picture together. There are many brushstrokes that look almost careless up close that are vital to the overall appearance of the picture.

In a way, a data model is very similar to an impressionist painting. A data model for a warehouse needs to be done very artfully so the individual pieces of information are carefully preserved. When bringing different sections of data together, it is important to place some key brushstrokes, such as customer level information, in a way that the entire data model assembles and "sings" together in harmony. I cannot stress the importance of keeping in mind the forest as well as the trees while designing a data model. There is no point getting lost in the forest while losing sight of the trees or concentrating on the trees too much while ignoring the forest. Too often, there are some vital pieces of information that are not captured at all or not captured in the same way, and this can hinder the way the data models come together. Here again, bringing together experts from several different areas in designing the data model would greatly help the overall process.

The key point here is that when building a data model, remember that you are creating an impressionist painting. The big picture (the keys that connect all the different data models together), the individual brushstrokes (vital pieces of information in each data model), as well as the placement of the small strokes in the right places (answering questions like "Are the key links across multiple models defined similarly?") are very important. Bad or hasty decisions in this area can affect the institution in a big way for a long time.

10. The Top Two Assets of Any Business Today Are People and Data

We live in a very different world compared to our forefathers. Throughout history, different talents have been valuable in different eras. Physical might was very important in human history for a long time. In the last century or so, knowledge has become supremely important. Dr. Jim Goodnight, CEO of SAS Institute Inc., which has been featured as one of the best companies to work for in multiple geographies, said,

"All my assets [meaning employees] walk out the door at 5:00. And it is my job to get them to come back the next day."[9] In knowledge-based businesses, the importance of people cannot be overestimated. The new emerging reality is that data is as important as people to a business if not more so. Everything that you want to know or are able to know about a customer is available in the interactions you have with the customer. I don't think the day is too far off when based on the dishes you order at a restaurant, intelligent systems can not only make a recommendation as to what deals should be marketed to you but also figure out the inherent insurance, health, credit, and other forms of risk that exist in you and recommend the appropriate remedies and actions to all parties concerned.

The first institutions that figure out a way to use data like this to understand the customer and take appropriate actions are going to be the winners. An organization that doesn't value its people or its data is not likely to prosper in this new economy. As we move deeper into the age of data dominance, it is imperative that each of us remember the ubiquitous nature of data. With respect to data and its use, we literally ain't seen nothing yet!

The key point to remember from this guideline is for organizations to value its people and data. Both of these ingredients are going to be essential to the success of any knowledge-based organization.

UNDERSTANDING TEXT DATA

These ten steps are crucial to succeeding in collecting data that is essential to effective behavioral modeling. Without tackling the data aspect of the problem, no level of sophistication in the models is likely to yield great results. The models are only as good as the data we put into them.

I have repeatedly referred to data in this chapter and may have misled the reader into believing that I am referring only to numbers. What I am referring to as data here consists of both numbers and text. Text data analysis has become very sophisticated, and text data is as precious as numbers in terms of understanding customer behavior. More and more of the data that is available today tends to be not just numbers but letters and detailed text in the form of notes that analysts take as well as data that is collected only as text—like merchant names, locations, and so on. There are many real-time scoring systems that use text-mining algorithms in real time and score text data along with numbers to decide what to do with a particular transaction with a customer. Text data in general tends to have more data entry errors, and it is important to fix these mistakes in real time, make sense of them, and use them to score algorithms.

For an example: A location like Philadelphia can be spelled and abbreviated in multiple ways, causing an interesting challenge in production. Let's say we have calculated the risk associated with transactions in the location Philadelphia. In order for us to apply the risk accurately to the incoming transaction that has happened in Philadelphia, we need to be able to identify that "Philadelphia," "Philly," "Philladelphia," "Filadelphia," "Filadelfia," and so on, are the same location. As you can see, one of the discrepancies is due to slang/abbreviation, and the rest of them are spelling/data entry errors. In order to allow the variable that calculates the risk associated with the location of this transaction, it will be important for all these words to mean the same location. However accurate our risk calculation, if this translation cannot be done effectively in production at the moment model scoring happens, the effectiveness of the calculation will be reduced significantly. A model is nothing but the sum total of a number of such calculations. The text-mining algorithms of today are very capable of dealing with such data issues. The truly sophisticated fraud detection systems of today have text-mining algorithms customized and embedded to function in real time. The raw material for this calculation can of course be done in an offline batch. However, the algorithms must execute in production very quickly.

Once the text data is understood, organized, arranged, and converted to numbers, the data is ready for use in the models just as regular data in numbers is. The only difference is that numbers arrive as numbers and are simple to use in production. Text data needs to be cleaned up and interpreted in high-throughput environments. Text mining, when combined correctly with traditional modeling methods, is capable of yielding rich rewards.

Most of the data captured today, especially on the Internet, is text data. Being able to make sense of text data in large quantities very quickly will be an important differentiator in the future. Banks have also seen a very high degree of shift in their transactions toward the Internet. The mobile channel is also playing a very important role in transactions. All of this tremendously increases the importance of text data in behavioral models.

Sir Ronald Aylmer Fisher, who is considered to be the greatest biologist since Darwin and one of the best statisticians who ever inhabited this planet, once said, "Modern statisticians are familiar with the notion that any finite body of data contains only a limited amount of information, on any point under examination; that this limit is set by the nature of the data themselves, and cannot be increased by any amount of ingenuity expended in their statistical examination; that the statistician's task, in fact, is limited to the extraction of the whole of the available information on any particular issue."[10] This clearly demonstrates that even the best modeling techniques cannot compensate for not having good data. The effectiveness of a data scientist's or statistician's job is determined by his/her ability to extract information from the data, and the amount of information available in the data is determined by the quality of the data. In other words, however good and skillful we are as craftsmen, we cannot make bricks without clay or an architectural wonder without good bricks. This fundamental principle is essential in any modeling area, and fraud models are no exception to this rule. Since there is so much data in the big data era, it is vital to figure out which pieces of information are important and to extract them correctly while preserving their integrity.

SUMMARY

One of my all my all-time favorite literary pieces is a poem called "If—" by Nobel Laureate Rudyard Kipling.[11] In this poem, he says,

If you can keep your head when all about you
Are losing theirs and blaming it on you,
If you can trust yourself when all men doubt you,
But make allowance for their doubting too;
If you can wait and not be tired by waiting,
Or being lied about, don't deal in lies,
Or being hated, don't give way to hating,

And yet don't look too good, nor talk too wise;

If you can dream—and not make dreams your master;
If you can think—and not make thoughts your aim;
If you can meet with Triumph and Disaster
And treat those two impostors just the same;
If you can bear to hear the truth you've spoken
Twisted by knaves to make a trap for fools,
Or watch the things you gave your life to, broken,
And stoop and build'em up with worn-out tools;

If you can make one heap of all your winnings
And risk it on one turn of pitch-and-toss,
And lose, and start again at your beginnings
And never breathe a word about your loss;
If you can force your heart and nerve and sinew
To serve your turn long after they are gone,
And so hold on when there is nothing in you
Except the Will which says to them: 'Hold on!'

If you can talk with crowds and keep your virtue,
Or walk with Kings—nor lose the common touch,
If neither foes nor loving friends can hurt you,
If all men count with you, but none too much;
If you can fill the unforgiving minute
With sixty seconds' worth of distance run,
Yours is the Earth and everything that's in it,
And—which is more—you'll be a Man, my son!

The great life lesson taught in this poem is important. Every time I read it (and I read it quite often), I get inspired, remembering that while surrounded by the ever-changing nature of life, staying steadfast to a few principles will distinguish you in the end. A subtle corollary I draw is that the fundamental principles stated here apply not only to people's personal lives but also to the lives of organizations. History has shown us repeatedly that organizations that have vision and stay steadfast to certain principles do extremely well in the long run. In the knowledge industry, if companies can truly value all the data they have, categorize the data, understand the data, preserve the data, use the data, maintain the data, and interpret the data, certainly the earth and everything that is in it related to their industry will belong to them. We already have indications that this is true. But in the future, I predict that this will become a universal truth. The race to do this is already on, and the companies that figure out how to do it right will emerge as the winners. It is no surprise that data science is emerging as one of the leading disciplines of this century.

CHAPTER **4**

Tackling Fraud: The Ten Commandments

Risk management is an exercise every one of us does voluntarily or involuntarily countless times during the course of our lives. Every decision we make involves some assessment of the risk involved. Even members of the animal kingdom do this on a regular basis. When an antelope in the African savannah decides whether it should go alone to have a drink of water in the nearby pond, it is making a calculated decision based on whether it can hear a lion roaring nearby, whether it is dark, whether it makes sense to go with the other deer to drink water or go alone. When a pedestrian is trying to cross a crowded New York street after the light has turned to a blinking Don't Walk, the decision to cross or not involves assessing the risk involved. We tend to draw from our personal experience and what we have been taught to make the decision. When a bank is trying to decide whether to approve a purchase for $1,500 that Joe Right is attempting at an electronics store, risk assessment is involved. While financial institutions are likely interested in managing all risk associated with their customers, fraud risk associated with certain products is one of the most important to the bank because of its direct and unpredictable impact on the bank's bottom line.

The one big difference between the situations of the antelope and pedestrian as opposed to the bank is the role that one's intuition can be allowed to play. It is very likely that the antelope and pedestrian have to make just that one crucial decision in the next few minutes. There is ample time and room for intuition in the decision. In the case of the bank, there are millions of transaction decisions that must be made in a day, and this tremendously increases the need to abstract and automate the processes around the decisions on these transactions. The process needs to be intelligent and systematic as well as nimble and fast. It is also crucial to be accurate in these decisions as the bank is focused on profitability, and fraud has a direct impact on profitability. There is more than one way in which a bad fraud decision affects the bottom line. The obvious one is the impact of allowing fraud to happen; the not-so-obvious one is mistakenly stopping non-fraud and upsetting customers.

The conditional risk and the perceived risk of an event distort reality to a great degree. In my life, I have come across at least a dozen people who absolutely will not travel by air regardless of what the circumstances are. The reason for their hesitation to travel in an airplane should be obvious. There is the perception of a tremendous amount of risk involved in air travel. Sometimes when people learn how much business travel I do in a year, their initial reaction of awe at the interesting nature of my job quickly turns to one of sympathy. Once they learn that I also travel on my own personal time, the sympathy deepens. While there are plenty of reasons one should be sympathetic toward frequent air travelers, I am not sure that the risk of air disaster should be one of the reasons. There is a much higher level of risk of personal injury or death in stepping out of the house and getting into a car to go somewhere than the risk in flying with a good commercial airline. The probability of getting into a traffic accident is much higher than the probability of a plane crashing. Yet I don't find people, at least not so far, who refuse to travel in a car. I realize that some of this is due to the inevitability of car travel in today's world and the familiarity of this mode of transport that we have gained over the last several decades. Some of this reaction is also because it is a lot easier for most people to avoid traveling in a plane but virtually impossible for people to avoid traveling in a vehicle. Some of the fear with air travel is accentuated by the media coverage when an air disaster happens—the events of 9/11 that sent shock waves throughout the world, for example. Some of the fear, however, is due to the conditional risk one takes on in air travel. In other words, when you are in the air, if the airplane experiences some difficulty, like a mechanical failure, things can get very bad very fast. This conditional risk is much higher than the risk one experiences when a car has a mechanical problem. However, people tend to forget that the probability of a mechanical failure in an airplane is really minuscule. The focus tends to be on the high conditional probability of disaster if there is some mechanical failure, while the condition itself, mechanical failure, is extremely rare.

The perception problem stated above can easily invade risk management and specifically fraud management departments. When that happens, the fraud management results are not likely to be optimal. I am reminded of a quote from Jay Abraham: "An amazing thing, the human brain. Capable of understanding incredibly complex and intricate concepts. Yet at times unable to recognize the obvious and simple."[1] I cannot even estimate the number of highly trained numbers people who get fixated on a small thing they found in the data and give it a lot more importance than it deserves. The obvious and simple concept of going after the biggest chunk of the risk to be tackled is something that is lost quite often. This seems to happen often even with domain experts.

One of my favorite authors, Stephen Covey,[2] talks about putting first things first in his book *The Seven Habits of Highly Effective People*. Putting first things first is important to follow in our day-to-day life, and it is also very important for an organization to follow. Prioritizing, and prioritizing *correctly*, is of paramount importance. Drawing on the rock in a glass jar analogy, once prioritization is done well, a lot can be accomplished not only with the big things but even with the list of small things that need to be taken care of. I am sure you have heard of the story of the optimal way to fill a glass jar with rocks, gravel, and sand. It illustrates the concept of how once we make room for the really big things in life, we will most likely be able to find room for the small things as well. It is important to fill the glass jar with the big rocks, small rocks, gravel, and sand in that order. The big rocks, small rocks, gravel, and sand are used as analogies for crucial, very important, important, and marginally important things in our life. The interesting quandary we are faced with in fraud risk management is this kind of classification.

Once I was in discussion with a fraud manager and was showing him what a fraud model could do to help him tackle fraud. He was very convinced that he was not in need of a model at all as he had some rules that were extremely good and could do a very good job of reducing false positives. He mentioned that his rules had a false positive ratio of 2:1 (meaning only two good accounts affected for every compromised [fraud] account, which is phenomenal for any fraud shop; typically most fraud shops operate in the 10:1 range and some fraud shops go as high as 20:1 in terms of false positive rate). He felt that he could do a lot better than the scores and was confident that he didn't really need scores. When we dug a little bit deeper into the numbers, we noticed that there were very few accounts that qualified under this strategy and so while the false positive rate looked very good, it didn't cover even 2 percent of the overall fraud the company experienced. After going through a few rounds of analysis, we understood that the fraud manager was very proud of this rule because he had contributed to developing it, and overall, the company was able to do very well because labor was relatively cheap and it was contacting significantly higher number of customers than what is normally needed to contain the overall losses. Unfortunately, this is a relatively common occurrence in fraud management.

If we look at dollars at risk quantified by banks, attrition risk (the risk of losing the customer and hence losing dollars) and credit risk (the risk of the customer not paying the bill) are far greater than fraud risk (the risk of fraudulent use of the bank product). Yet fraud risk needs to be closely managed. While credit risk is looked at as the cost of doing business, and attrition risk cannot be avoided when there is competition (especially in this day and age when customers' expectations of banks are high), fraud risk is a piece of the overall risk picture that should and can be managed closely. Fraud risk, if addressed expertly, can yield significant results right away. Managing fraud risk involves the same good old principles of always doubting one's intuition and going with one's intuition only when data also supports it, and solving the big solvable problems first and avoiding getting stuck in a narrow corner with minutiae that may not matter.

Some of the elements an organization needs to manage fraud risk effectively are process related; some are mind-set related; some depend on how objective we can be in keeping our eyes on the goal of managing. Based on my experience of working with a number of large banks and showing them how to tackle fraud more effectively, here are the "Ten Commandments" that I believe can help any risk management department. Each one of these principles will require concentrated and focused work by the entire organization. There is an African proverb that says, "If you want to go fast, go alone; if you want to go far, go together." It will be extremely important for everyone to go together in this endeavor to make huge advancements in fraud management.

My ten commandments for fraud management:

1. Data: Garbage in; garbage out.
2. No documentation? No change!
3. Key employees are not a substitute for good documentation.
4. Rules: More doesn't mean better.
5. Score: Never rest on your laurels.
6. Score + rules = winning strategy.
7. Fraud is everyone's problem.
8. Continual assessment is the key.
9. Fraud control systems: If they rest, they rust.
10. Continual improvement: The cycle never ends.

1. DATA: GARBAGE IN; GARBAGE OUT

In the book *Passages from the Life of a Philosopher*, Charles Babbage says: "On two occasions I have been asked, 'Pray, Mr. Babbage, if you put into the machine wrong figures, will the right answers come out?'. . . I am not able rightly to apprehend the kind of confusion of ideas that could provoke such a question."[3] "Garbage in; garbage out" is a classic term in computer science that is used to show that a machine cannot produce the right answers if the wrong information is put into it; a computer simply processes the data presented to it and gives an answer. This is true of any data-driven algorithm development and execution as well. "Garbage in; gospel out" is an expression used today to show that since is it very difficult to go after the source data that allows computers to give us answers, we have to accept what the computer outputs as gospel. This may be true of some of the results that a computer produces, but it does not have to be the case for data-driven risk management systems. It is possible to have very good controls in place for defining, categorizing, and monitoring data. It is also possible to monitor data on a regular basis to ensure the data captured makes sense and that the data is consistent with what we expect to see. For every data-driven risk management system, monitoring the fields that are fed into the solution regularly is not a luxury but a requirement for the healthy upkeep of the system. Some of the most sophisticated systems currently have this daily monitoring built in.

Production monitoring of data in fraud detection systems is important. It is implicit that monitoring data in any production system is important. Data is the raw material for all the rules and models developed to manage fraud. If the raw material is flawed, the conclusions drawn based on the raw material will almost certainly be flawed. In the previous chapter, the detailed steps to a good data environment are listed. In order to create such an environment, a mind-set and culture that treats data to be of supreme importance have to be inculcated and nurtured. In a number of environments, even if the data flowing through a production system is of good quality, the good-quality data is not necessarily the data that gets captured for rebuilding models in the future. There is significant discrepancy in data simply due to how the data is captured. It is very encouraging to see systems that are complete in terms of scoring, applying rules, alert management, data capture, and reporting. Such systems are likely to improve the quality of models in a very significant way. Fraud detection systems that include all of these in a complete package are the way to go.

With banks, a very common mistake is to value any data derived from "monetary" transactions well above data from "other" transactions. For example, if a customer withdrew cash from an ATM, this transaction is typically viewed as quite important, and the details of the transaction are well preserved. This certainly makes a lot of sense. However, sometimes there are other transactions that are equally if not more important. Let's take a specific example. A "balance inquiry" transaction in the debit card world is typically treated as an "other" or "non monetary" transaction. A balance inquiry transaction immediately followed by an ATM cash withdrawal is generally not very risky from a fraud management perspective. This basically means that the customer is checking to see if there is enough balance in the account before making cash withdrawal. However, if there is a balance inquiry transaction followed by a couple of hours of no activity and then a point of sale (POS) transaction (especially in certain categories) follows, this scenario tends to be risky. (POS transactions in these categories not preceded by the balance inquiry transaction don't tend to be that risky.) If the balance inquiry transactions are not recorded very carefully in the historic data, there will certainly be a significant impact on the efficacy of the modeling exercises. In production, it is important to report these "other" transactions in as timely a fashion as possible. A lot of fraud today originates in "other" transactions, and it is important to monitor these transactions.

Sometimes the impact of not keeping track of a particular type of transaction can be more widespread than just affecting a particular product from a fraud perspective—for example, a fraud compromise where Jack Wrong, our fraudster, managed to install a camera that watches every ATM cash withdrawal. The debit card number and the PIN entered by the customers are carefully recorded by this camera. Jack Wrong manages to produce the physical card and knows the PIN number. Using these, he can easily withdraw cash from the ATM. Instead, he decides to do something more serious. He goes to an ATM and, using the card and the PIN, he requests a "mini-statement." A mini-statement typically tells you the last few withdrawals made on the account. Why is this important? Some banks use the verification of these transactions as a way to authenticate the customer. With the sensitive information Jack Wrong has managed to collect on the account, he calls the bank and asks for a funds transfer to a different account in a different bank. The bank asks him for the PIN, asks him to verify the last few transactions (which he can do easily using the information obtained in the mini-statement), and then it allows him to transfer funds to his account. This scenario can be mitigated by employing a more detailed and sophisticated authentication system that verifies a number of details on the account.

Interestingly, in this particular example, there is not much damage to the debit card product from a fraud perspective. However, using the information skimmed on the debit card, the fraudster has managed to gain access to entire checking and savings accounts, and this can cause a lot more damage. This fraud will not be recorded as debit card fraud, and in most systems, the link between the usage of the debit card at the ATM and this type of fraud won't be known. Traditionally, from a "debit card silo" point of view, fraud solutions lean toward de emphasizing information that may not be relevant to the product in consideration (debit card in this example) from a fraud perspective (technically, the fraud episode in this example is associated with and counted as checking account fraud and not debit card fraud). As sophisticated fraud management solutions spanning multiple products and detecting fraud from an enterprise fraud perspective gain prominence in the marketplace, virtually all pieces of information become very valuable. So, from an enterprise fraud modeling perspective, having information on the mini-statements is just as important as the monetary transactions are. If the mini-statement information is simply not available in the historic data or if some of the mini-statement requests are not recorded in the historic data, the situation is far from ideal. The system will not be nearly as accurate as it could be if this information was available.

There are a number of examples of other types of non monetary transactions that are crucial to dealing with fraud. For example, address change, phone number change, or any significant change is extremely important from an "account take-over" fraud perspective. Fundamentally, there are different levels of data that could be missing from the historic data. Sometimes it is the level of granularity that is required in the data (not having information on some key ways in which the transaction was made, for instance) that is missing. Sometimes transactions are completely dropped from certain days or certain hours. Sometimes certain types of transactions are not recorded as carefully as they should be. All of these types of omissions can be very detrimental to the health of the data. The health of the data is crucial to how good the models are, both today and in the future. If there is an environment where everyone cares about data, it will be a rich and fertile environment for fraud models to flourish as well. While the importance of this data from a model development perspective is obvious, transactions such as mini-statements are also important to verify with the customer at the time of the fraud to gain a complete picture of how the fraud got perpetrated.

To date, the enterprise fraud problem has been tackled marginally at best by most financial institutions. The number of ways in which fraudsters can use the loopholes in the system is mind boggling and is getting worse, not better. By strengthening the data enterprise, great strides can be made toward effective enterprise fraud management. In order to fully utilize some of the sophisticated fraud solutions available now and in the future, it will be important to treat all data as important.

In many banks, the knowledge that missing data can have a huge impact in the downstream process is simply nonexistent. Once this knowledge becomes commonplace in banks, much progress will be made.

2. NO DOCUMENTATION? NO CHANGE!

A common pitfall in any data environment is lack of documentation. Before proceeding to talk about documentation, I want to clarify what I am referring to here. I am not talking about documenting programs. This is useful only to a certain degree, and often, it can get too voluminous to be useful. What I am referring to is documentation of data field changes. Understanding data field changes is essential for any analytical fraud management process to function well. Very often, there is not a central area in a bank that one can go to and understand all the changes that a particular field has undergone. I have seen this to be the case even in large-scale data warehouses with detailed metadata layers. Metadata typically describes the means, purpose, time and date of creation, definition, the author, where the data resides, and so on. Metadata, of course, is very useful. But there are issues that arise as the data warehouse grows and changes. As a database grows, typically new fields need to be stored, and these fields were not envisioned as part of the original database. One common way to accommodate new fields is by repurposing already defined fields. But when fields are repurposed, all too often the metadata is not updated. This leads to a lot of confusion and unnecessary work later on.

Very often, in a database environment, people derive a lot of meaning about a field from its name. This has become a very common practice in database environments. In the immortal work *Romeo and Juliet* by Shakespeare, Juliet says, "What's in a name? That which we call a rose by any other name would smell as sweet"[4] to Romeo. This beautiful statement, however, does not apply to field names in a database. When dealing with data, a rose by a different name is not the same as a rose. Very often, field names become the proxy documentation for the fields. In a database, everything might be "in the name," and that becomes a problem. Let's say we decide to store "customer type" in a two-digit character field. If this field gets repurposed to denote "card type" of the card issued, it is very easy to confuse two completely different fields. The confusion is made worse if there is overlap or complete match in the characters used to represent the two fields. Let's say both fields take on the same values A, B, C, D, E, and F, and let's say the field became "card type" instead of "customer type" on March 1, 2011. After March 1, 2011, the integrity of this field is questionable. Most likely, unless a well-versed and curious data scientist looks at the data and figures out that there is some problem, the underlying data could be rendered completely useless. Sometimes this type of change is never uncovered during a modeling project, and sometimes it is found after wasting a number of cycles. This seems like a very simple and almost silly problem but it is extremely prevalent.

With the level of sophistication that is possible in today's documentation tools, one would think that it is very straightforward to completely document all the changes a field has undergone and make all of that information available to the end user. On observation, though, we would see that it is not the case. The documentation tools are not the limiting factor in most cases. It is the mind-set that documenting the field is an option as opposed to a requirement that is the limiting factor. Documentation of fields and what they mean at various points of time during the life of the field is not an option for any bank; it is absolutely essential to protecting the assets of the bank; in this case, the asset is the data.

The situation can be even worse in large-scale data environments on the mainframe that may or may not be database driven. The layout is often documented but the fields and the field values are not. Changes in field content are often unearthed by some serious detective work by a few people working on a specific project. Often knowledge thus gained is not propagated across multiple projects. In general, other than the programs written to be self-documenting, there is not much information available about data mapping decisions that were made, let alone why these decisions were made—which in itself could be very useful information. Data mapping, documentation, and change monitoring are as important as using advanced techniques to build models. An environment that takes this seriously and executes on this will likely make great strides in fraud management as well.

The obvious reason for documentation is to ensure smooth transfer of key field information throughout the entire organization. There is a nice side benefit to having an environment that encourages documentation. The process that gets organized around documentation will naturally result in better dialogue and a better thought out process for changing the meaning and content of fields. In most banking environments, this is done by a few people who may or may not have insight into the overall implications of making such changes. The importance of some of the changes sometimes is not immediately obvious. When a process is implemented to systematically understand and document changes, this introduces order, and that helps improve the overall thinking about changes as well. Addressing this challenge efficiently is essential to progress. Doing so also helps educate the different departments on what is important to the multiple players involved in this exercise.

Every system looks nearly perfect when it is first assembled. However, with passage of time, it becomes more and more flawed. It is interesting to look at the notion of entropy as we discuss this. Thermodynamics is a fascinating field, and the laws of thermodynamics have long held my awe and interest. The ideas are simple but they are time tested and valuable in real-world situations. Even though thermodynamics is a field dealing with heat, energy, and motion, the laws of thermodynamics go way beyond these fundamental concepts and can be applied broadly. My favorite one is the second law of thermodynamics, which deals with the entropy of a system not in thermal equilibrium. The entropy of such a system is always increasing. We can also interpret this as energy never staying still but always getting dispersed or distributed. There are many subtle interpretations of this law. As an organization grows, the structure and the cohesiveness of the information becomes diluted; additional fields are introduced that capture additional data that was not originally collected, replace an existing field, rendering that existing field redundant, or extend the meaning of existing fields; also, the scope of an existing field may be extended, allowing it to take an additional range of values. If effective controls are not in place, it is even possible for additional fields to be introduced that are duplicates of already existing fields. If we measure the entropy of a system by the number of changes done to the fields, the entropy (which can be thought of as a measure of loss of information) increases. An effective organization needs to keep entropy increases to a minimum to avoid loss of useful information. The larger the system, the more it must be protected.

In the data world, when there was a movement toward smaller databases and away from large mainframe and similar environments, one of the benefits touted was a more organized way of information sharing. This proved to be true for a short period of time with the introduction of the metadata layer and a systematic way of keeping information organized. (I am not suggesting there was no metadata in the mainframe environment; just that there was a higher focus to document data diligently in the database environments compared than in the mainframe environments.) The small databases grew into large data warehouses that grew into giant data warehouses.

However, when I observe in today's world the move toward cloud computing and thin-client access, I feel things have come full circle. Isn't cloud computing somewhat similar to mainframe computing? Isn't thin client similar to the terminal access we had with mainframes? I am not trying to undervalue all the improvements that we have experienced in all these years, but processes and systems have a natural way of evolution and sometimes we travel a full circle and arrive at a set of problems similar to our problems at the beginning. In other words, history repeats itself.

Why is this important to what we are discussing? As much as the nature of data storage changes, the challenges with understanding, organizing, and retaining the knowledge of data stay the same. I am not really sure if we handle these challenges much better today than we did before. It is best to address some of these challenges effectively no matter what level of evolution the organization is at. Some of the ways in which we attempt to solve the problems might change, but the problems (at least some of them) don't seem to change. The fundamental guiding principles remain the same. Any data-driven organization should take documentation of changes very seriously and do it diligently, on a very regular basis. There is no silver bullet to address this problem. Like a lot of things in life, it is systematic hard work.

3. KEY EMPLOYEES ARE NOT A SUBSTITUTE FOR GOOD DOCUMENTATION

We live in unprecedented times. Never before has the human workforce been as valued as it is now. This statement may not be true in all parts of the world and across different industries. However, what we are witnessing today in terms of people being valued by companies is a phenomenon never witnessed in recorded history of the period before the second half of the 20th century. The knowledge industry is a great example of this. If we look even a few decades into the past, I am not sure if this was true. The reliance of companies on a small group of employees and their contributions to the company is a key differentiator of the times we live in. Not all the creativity and the ideas in an employee's head can be written down and preserved. Some employees do truly become irreplaceable no matter how much as we believe in the saying "No one is indispensable."

While what I have said about companies' reliance on employees is true about some key functions, the reliance of financial institutions on employees for information goes well beyond what is perhaps needed by these institutions in some areas. Data documentation is one such area. We have seen at length how crucial data assets are to any financial institution. When the nature of data undergoes changes (field definitions or content) in a bank, very little of that information is documented. Most of the information is stored in the heads of some key employees, and these key employees are generally not involved in every data management project. There is a significant level of detail that is left to chance (there is a discussion on this topic in Chapter Three ["In God We Trust. The Rest Bring Data!"]), and it is up to the person analyzing the data to find the anomalies and question them. The anomalies could be in the form of missing data, change in data field definition, change in the content of the fields, and so on. If the person conducting the analysis is not very thorough and misses finding these anomalies, they end up never being rationalized for the particular project. I cannot tell you the number of times we have gone round and round in circles with a data anomaly that bothered a data scientist and finally, the reply comes from the client—"Oh yeah! We made that change sometime in April and unfortunately we don't have too many more details." When incomplete information is used to build a data-driven system, the system will not be able to function at an adequate level. The cycle of incomplete information gets propagated to future decisions, and the cost of such missing data can be high. Often we don't know what we don't know. There is significant opportunity that is lost by the banks due to missing data.

As someone who has been involved in hundreds of data-intensive projects dealing with data from multiple banks to detect fraud, predict credit risk, predict best marketing offers, and the like, it is hard to believe how much of this information about data is discovered by repeated insistence of a few data scientists and analysts and how much of the information resides in the (sometimes fading) memories of key employees at the banks. While reliance on employees in the area of advanced modeling or financial forecasting or complex IT design makes a lot of sense, it does not make a lot of sense to have this reliance in simple data documentation matters. A culture of documentation and sharing of knowledge on a consistent basis in matters of data changes must be instituted, developed, and nurtured. Just as is true with any change in an organization, this will take time and dedicated effort by all to accomplish. One nice fringe benefit of accomplishing this would be to free up the time of these key employees to work on more productive projects for the bank. Some banks have done a better job of tackling this challenge compared to others, and the speed at which these banks can execute on projects is also significantly higher than other institutions.

While the focus of this book has been the challenges faced by banks in the area of fraud, I suspect the challenges are shared by multiple industries that can all benefit from this cultural shift. Just as many underdeveloped economies leapfrogged the wired phone phase directly to cell phones, industries that are on the verge of using data heavily hopefully will bypass the lack-of-documentation stage and have a healthy appreciation of the importance of data from day one.

4. RULES: MORE DOESN'T MEAN BETTER

As it is with children or pets, having too many rules is generally counterproductive. Too many rules tend to confuse them. Interestingly, fraud management systems are no different. Having too many fraud rules causes a lot of confusion instead of solving the problem.

Let's define what a rule is in this context. Any fraud management exercise typically starts with a domain expert observing how fraud has happened. Based on seeing enough examples of fraud, the expert devises rules that can stop fraud in its the tracks the next time around. One rule could be: "If the transaction amount is greater than or equal to $500 and the transaction time is between 12 midnight and 4 a.m., then block the transaction." Let's say this qualifies 500 transactions to be blocked on a given night, of which 25 transactions turn out to be fraudulent. Another domain expert observes that transactions that are over $600 in certain merchant category code (MCC) categories to be risky. Let's say he writes a rule: "If the transaction is greater than or equal to $600 and the MCC category is 'casino,' 'jewelry,' or 'electronics,' then block the transaction." Let's say this qualifies 1,200 transactions on a given day, of which 40 transactions turn out to be fraudulent. Let's say that if we observe the transactions only between 12 midnight and 4 a.m. (which the previous rule attempts to identify), the fraud rate changes to only 25 transactions among 600 that qualify in this pool. If there was a rule written that says all three conditions must be satisfied—transaction amount greater than $600, transactions happening between 12 midnight and 4 a.m., and MCC categories representing "casino," "jewelry," or "electronics," this could have brought down the number of transactions to, say, 150 with 23 transactions being fraudulent. This fraud rate is much more desirable than what the individual rules have been able to achieve on their own.

However, information on two such fraud rules working more effectively together is generally not analyzed and understood. If there is a rule on high-dollar transactions at night, it is typically not examined systematically to see if the rule can be made a lot better by adding additional elements to it. In this particular example, there is only a small overlap between the two rules in terms of the non-fraud transactions but very significant overlap in terms of the fraud transactions. If both rules are run separately and we consider the results only at night, the total false positive transactions (non-fraud customers who will have to be called to verify transactions) is (500 − 25) + (600 − 25) = 1,050. This is the number of calls that have to made to identify 23 (fraudulent transactions that overlap) + 2 (fraudulent that are specific to the first rule only) + 2 (fraudulent transactions that are specific to the second rule only) = 29 total. However, if the two rules had been combined, we could have identified 23 of the 29 frauds while making just 150 calls, which is 1/7 the number of calls we would have to make otherwise. The example given here is a very simple one. Typical overlaps involve significantly more complex rules, and hence systematic analysis and understanding is a bit harder to conduct on a regular basis.

Rules-based systems generally do not lend themselves easily to looking at the overlaps and conflicts between rules. Take the example above and extrapolate the situation to an environment with 1,000 rules. (This is not an exaggeration, by the way; fraud management departments that rely solely on rules-based systems typically have well over 1,000 rules.) It becomes quite obvious to us that it is simply not possible to systematically analyze these rules on a regular basis.

Model-based systems have the capability to combine all of these attributes (transaction amount is large, time of the transaction is not the regular hours, transaction category is more risky) and utilize them in a nonlinear model such as a neural network. Neural networks are capable of assessing and allowing interactions between variables in the model without much human intervention or "tweaking" of the model. There is a lot to be gained from such systems. In the beginning, neural networks were simply used as black boxes where a number of variables are thrown into the kitchen sink model, and the network is allowed to understand the intricacies of the relationships and output a number that can be interpreted to be the probability of fraud. Such systems proved to be much better than rules-based systems, but systems that exploit the behavior-based segments in populations and models that thoroughly understand the role that variables play provide much better fraud detection. Some of the more sophisticated behavior-based segments not only consider what sort of behavior is exhibited currently but also how the behavior evolved. Such systems with behavior-based segments and different models for each segment have been introduced in the recent past and have far superior fraud detection performance. More discussion on the different types of analytical methods for fraud models is provided in Chapter Seven ("Fraud Analytics: We Are Just Scratching the Surface").

A very interesting customer behavior change has been observed in the last 15 years or so. Back in the mid-1990s, when simple neural network–based systems were introduced to detect fraud in credit cards, I remember getting calls from card issuers. While most of the transactions they were verifying were not fraudulent, I remember feeling a sense of security that my bank was watching the transactions on my behalf and I wasn't irritated by calls from the banks verifying my transactions. Now, however, I get a number of calls verifying transactions (that are also not fraudulent and were made by me) and I tend to get irritated by the bank's inability to understand that I made these transactions and not the fraudster. There are stories in the industry of some big issuers losing a lot of customers partly due to these repeated customer annoyance calls. Consumer expectations are at a higher level today and hence it is important to have fraud management systems that produce as few fraud alerts as possible. In order to achieve this, a system based on domain expertise or simple analytics-driven rules will not suffice. More rules don't mean better results; they generally mean worse, sometimes *much* worse, results.

5. SCORE: NEVER REST ON YOUR LAURELS

What is a fraud score? A fraud score can be calculated in a number of different ways. It could be a simple system that gives a score based on weighting a few attributes. For example, a score could be: Everyone starts with a score of 500; if the transaction amount is greater than $500, add 50 to the score for every $100 increase till $1,000; add 25 to the score for every increase of $200 till $5,000; stop when the amount hits $10,000. Scoring systems were common 20 or so years ago. After this, a number of model-based systems were introduced, with increasing complexity as well as effectiveness. Linear regression models were built using different attributes weighted in different (data-driven) ways, and the final output (typically in the range of 0.001 to 0.999) was converted into a score by some translation of the final output. A simple translation of the score could be to multiply the output by 1,000. There are more complex transformations possible to convert certain scores to certain odds of seeing fraud (say a score of 800 means odds of 20:1; in other words, if we accumulate a group of accounts with fraud episode scoring above 800, there will be one that will represent a fraud episode for every 20 non-fraud accounts encountered).

If the comparison is done between model-based systems and rules-based systems, even simple models are likely to yield better results as models consider multiple factors simultaneously while rules consider only a few attributes at a time. In other words, models tend to have a bird's-eye view of the problem while rules have blinders on and have a narrow view of a certain set of frauds or a certain type of fraud. However, as a model gets more complex, the effectiveness of the model also increases.

Neural networks are good at modeling nonlinear phenomena. They yield far superior detection of fraud compared to linear or logistic regression models. Some risk phenomena do tend to be linear in nature. For a simple example of this, let's say we are measuring the number of units a manufacturing plant can produce. Let's say that producing one unit requires raw material A and B, and enough machines to make the unit. Let's say that the manufacturing plant has 100 machines. Let's say one unit requires two units of A and three units of B and one machine for 10 minutes. Let's assume the machines are in good condition and work nonstop for 10 hours a day. In a day, in the range of 1 to 6,000, units can be produced as long as we have 12,000 quantities of A and 18,000 quantities of B. If we were to plot the relationship of the units produced to a combination of the time used—A and B—a linear relationship would emerge. Suppose we build a model that predicts the number of units we can produce for a certain amount of A and B we have available; the model again will emerge as a linear model as there is not much nonlinearity in the problem.

However, real-world situations of fraud management are not the same. Let's assume higher dollar amounts are riskier from a fraud perspective. The risk doesn't keep increasing proportionally to the amount. In other words, there is never a real-world situation where $2,000 is exactly twice as risky as $1,000. Also, the risk tapers off or drops off beyond a certain level. For example, if the amount of a transaction is over $10,000, there is minimal fraud risk as very rarely does any fraudster attempt a transaction over a few thousand dollars at a time. I have oversimplified the previous example. In a typical fraud model, the prediction is based on has tens of attributes (or independent variables). Each one of the attributes has a certain relationship to the fraud target that is nonlinear but uniquely nonlinear. In other words, the way in which the amount of the transaction varies with the fraud risk is not the same as the way the time of the transaction varies. To accommodate all these variables and ensure they are all valuable in the model, their unique relationships to fraud risk must be well understood.

Actually, it gets more complex than understanding each variable's nonlinear relationship to fraud risk. To reduce false positives (and unnecessary dollars spent on calling customers who were not defrauded), it is quite important to understand the nonlinear relationships *across* these different variables. In other words, it is important to understand the relationship between higher dollar amounts and fraud risk as well as the time of the transaction and fraud risk. It is also very important to understand while higher dollar amount transactions (variable A) and transactions happening in the midnight–to 4–a.m. range (Variable B) are risky, higher dollar transactions happening in the midnight–to 4–a.m. time range are even more risky. Back propagation neural networks with a hidden layer include such interactions automatically the models. This reduces the false positives compared to simpler models.

There is yet another layer of complexity that can be introduced by understanding the nuances of how this relationships of variables A and B described above are different among cash users and non-cash users.

We could differentiate between cash users who have always been cash users versus cash users who have become cash users because of some life stage change. Sophisticated systems today are capable of looking at not just where a customer is today but how the customer got there. All of these are layers of complexity that progressively improve detecting fraud.

So far, we discussed the relationships of various variables to fraud risk and how different modeling methodologies consider and include them for better fraud detection performance. While fraud is inherently hard to detect, increased sophistication in fraud is also something that dictates improvement in the detection systems. Gone are the days when fraud was mostly opportunistic in nature. Nowadays, it is conducted by organized crime rings. Expanding on the skimming example from the "Data: Garbage In; Garbage Out" section earlier in this chapter, besides using the skimmed data to break into checking and savings accounts, there could also be a crime ring that takes over the number and the PINs systematically, produces the physical cards, and, after checking online to make sure cards are valid, uses each card to withdraw a small dollar amount—say $100—from a few remote ATM terminals. It may be a small fraud loss on each card, but if that fraud is committed on 10,000 cards, all of a sudden the bank has lost $1,000,000 in a couple of hours. Worse yet, the fraud detection systems that are looking for a pattern of fraud emerging based on the cardholder will not be able to detect a $100 ATM withdrawal. A $100 ATM withdrawal is likely totally consistent with what the customers typically do.

In the above case, it is important for good fraud detection systems to observe the activity at the ATM terminals in real time and understand quickly that while these transactions may be totally in character for the individual customers, they are out of character for the particular ATM terminal and hence need to be blocked. Luckily, there are systems that are capable of doing this today; using scoring systems that look at the fraud episode from a multidimensional point of view (the ATM terminal is just one of many entities that need to be modeled in real time) will be key to addressing fraud effectively. Looking at deviations in account behavior alone to detect fraud isn't cutting edge anymore. It is becoming extremely important to model and understand multiple entities in real time. It is also important to use up-to-the-millisecond information on a number of these entities, not just the customer.

Unfortunately, as fraud management systems get sophisticated, fraudsters also get sophisticated. While resting on one's laurels has not been a good idea since ancient Greek times, it can be very costly from a fraud management perspective. Scoring processes have to keep on improving in order to tackle fraud effectively.

6. SCORE + RULES = WINNING STRATEGY

I sang the praises of scoring in the previous section and how using more advanced modeling techniques is likely to yield better results. While this is absolutely true, I do not want to leave the reader with the impression that only scores are important and we don't need any operational rules in fraud management. Rules are extremely important to use with the scores.

Operationalizing scores and using them effectively in production is as important as building great fraud scores for fraud management. The world's best models are totally useless if they cannot be used effectively in production to manage fraud. It is essential for fraud analysts to know what to do when the score is above a score threshold. Let's assume a score above 800 is risky. Does this mean every transaction scoring above 800 should be blocked right away and until the customer is contacted, no further transactions are allowed? That is not true. Even when the score is risky, we cannot assume the same treatment will be applied to all transactions scoring above a certain threshold. Banks may be less willing to inconvenience certain high-net-worth individuals as opposed to others. The value of the overall relationship might play a role in the treatment applied.

Another big shift in the last decade in fraud is the proportion of casual fraud as opposed to the systematic takeover of accounts. When a fraud analyst is calling to verify a transaction, if he/she is talking to the customer who is also the perpetrator of fraud, it requires a certain amount of sophistication on the part of the analyst to tease out the information from the customer. Let's consider the following scenario: Our fraudster Jack Wrong has managed to acquire the account number, PIN, and address of Joe Right. With this information, he calls the bank and asks for an address change and a phone number change. He has effectively shifted the address of the account to his address. Using this information, he also requests a spending limit increase. Let's say the bank grants it, thinking it is with Joe Right, who is a very good customer. Jack Wrong gets the new account details, knows the balance, and has also managed to get the credit card under the account reissued to the new address. He starts charging against the card but he is in no hurry, unlike traditional fraudsters. Typical fraud episodes only last a few days but in this case, he knows he has at least a month, probably a few months. He can take his time and shop to his heart's content. Let's say that in the middle of this string of transactions some of which seem like what Joe Right might make but some of which look totally uncharacteristic, the fraud management system scores a transaction high, and it creates a case. If this is handed off to a regular "smile and dial" fraud analyst who calls the phone number on the account (which is Jack Wrong's phone number) and wants to verify the transactions, he/she is very likely to verify all of them easily as there is an eager customer at the other end of the phone who wants to prolong the life of the card and the associated cash as much as possible.

In the above case, it would be very important to classify this transaction as one to be handled carefully. It should be given to a more experienced fraud analyst who can smell that something is not right and probe more to verify additional details so that the account takeover situation can be discovered and addressed. In order to deal with situations like this, it would be essential to have rules that take the sophistication of the scores and convert them into something actionable. If the score is above 800 and a certain set of criteria is met, route the account to fraud analyst X instead of analyst Y, who has not been trained to handle more complex fraud cases. Taking this concept further, it is very encouraging to see that some of fraud detection systems don't just stop with providing effective fraud scores—they are also able effectively to predict the *type* of fraud likely to occur.

There are a number of other operational considerations in managing fraud: whether to queue a transaction at this time or not; whether to block the card or not. Also, there may be certain types of fraud that happen over a very short period of time that a set of rules can handle more effectively than a score can. Rules are also needed to input "hot lists" (information gathered from the industry on accounts that have been compromised). If a particular zip code needs to be watched closely on a given day, rules will be needed to handle such exceptions over a short period of time.

A sophisticated scoring system combined with a limited set of rules to take into account operational considerations is the winning combination to address fraud. Having too many rules can water down the fraud management system, but even the best scores are not very useful unless the operational use of the scores is streamlined with some carefully crafted rules to maximize benefits.

7. FRAUD: IT IS EVERYONE'S PROBLEM

In the book *The Five People You Meet in Heaven,*[5] Mitch Albom writes, "There are no random acts. . . . We are all connected. . . . You can no more separate one life from another than you can separate a breeze from the wind. . . ." In this work of fiction—which was on the *New York Times* best-seller list—the author describes the after-death experience of an 83-year-old man who dies and in the afterlife finds out that heaven is the place where you meet five people who were in your life, affected your life, or were affected by your life. Notwithstanding the metaphysical nature of this fiction, there are some interesting applications of the ideas in the book to the area of fraud management.

When we look at the life cycle of how data flows and decisions are made on a customer's transactions in a bank, the hope is that there are no random acts. While this applies to the entire life cycle of the customer's dealings with the bank, let's consider only the fraud management portion of it. Just to make things interesting, let's assume we are talking about enterprise fraud management. Every little bit of information we drop on the floor, every transaction that doesn't get recorded, every rule that doesn't get used right, every score that doesn't get used optimally, every fraud analyst that doesn't get trained well has an impact on the overall fraud management picture.

In order to manage fraud effectively at the enterprise level, an organization needs to have a fraud management mind-set from the lowest levels of the totem pole to the highest levels. Fraud management is not just the fraud manager's (who has the fraud line item in his budget) problem. It is everyone's problem. As fraud gets more complex, more innovative, and more sophisticated, it will be important for banks to stay a step ahead of the fraudsters. This will require a lot of education, goal setting, and process improvement to accomplish. It will also be important to communicate successes in fraud management to the entire organization so that everyone learns from the effective strategies.

Effective fraud management is about finding the worst problem in the overall functioning of the fraud detection system and continually fixing the problem. Frank A. Clark once said, "Everyone is trying to accomplish something big, not realizing that life is made up of little things."[6] This statement is absolutely true of fraud management as well. In order to achieve something big in fraud management, it is very important to take care of the little things, and take care of them on a very regular basis. In fraud management, attention to detail is as important as understanding the big picture.

8. CONTINUAL ASSESSMENT IS THE KEY

In Chapter Two ("Quantifying Loss: Whose Loss Is It Anyway?"), we discussed the censored nature of the fraud problem. Perhaps as a result of this, the general understanding of how well a fraud management system is functioning is much worse than the understanding of other forms of risk. One other issue with fraud is also its changing nature. A really good fraud detection system could be installed and, immediately after, if there is an outbreak of fraud in general, it is hard to separate what if any was caused by the system as opposed to the environment. Understanding the metrics used to measure fraud and assessing these metrics on a regular basis are both crucial to fraud management. In Chapter Eight ("The Proof of the Pudding May Not Be in the Eating"), we discuss in detail the best ways to assess and understand fraud scoring systems.

It is equally important also to understand whether fraud analysts are functioning as expected. Quite often, fraud management units do not have established ways of training fraud analysts and there is not enough uniformity in how the fraud analysts handle cases. It will be extremely important to continually assess and plug any holes identified in the entire process. Continual ongoing assessment of the system and systematically plugging holes will yield superior results over a period of time. Sometimes plugging these holes involves establishing new processes or updating existing processes; sometimes it involves performing a complete overhaul of the fraud detection system; sometimes it involves being nimble and reacting to new fraud trends faster. All of the above require that the problem with the system has been identified appropriately. Continual assessment is a key ingredient to achieve this. At the very minimum, fraud management systems should provide ongoing continual information on how well they are functioning without requiring significant work on the part of the user.

9. FRAUD CONTROL SYSTEMS: IF THEY REST, THEY RUST

If we look at the nature of fraud in banks over the last two decades, today looks nothing like what was happening 15 to 20 years ago. The regulatory environment has changed tremendously, and this has resulted in liability shifts in certain fraud types. Fraudsters have become extremely sophisticated, and so fraud is harder to detect. Due to a lot of commerce moving to the Internet, fraud has become much more impersonal than before. If the system the banks are using is based on fraud detection from two decades ago, the results achieved will be suboptimal. Fraud control systems have to evolve and change with the times, and the changes have to happen in an agile fashion.

Including new data feeds in the existing systems should be done in a seamless fashion. If a particular data feed—for example, mobile deposits—is introduced, the data has to be able to enter the fraud management system, be recognized by the system, and get included in the fraud decisioning process without a long wait. A number of existing fraud management systems require a total overhaul in order for new data feeds to be introduced into the fraud management process. This is simply not feasible in the current environment of effective fraud management. With the technology that is available today—which is far better than what was available a couple of decades ago—new data feeds can be included in the fraud management system in a relatively straightforward manner.

In order to become aware of such systems, it is important for fraud management groups to constantly look to improve their fraud detection systems. This can become a bit tricky in large production environments. However, this is going to be vital to managing the emerging fraud landscape.

10. CONTINUAL IMPROVEMENT: THE CYCLE NEVER ENDS

This cycle of assessment and revamping never ends. This is probably true of a number of risk management systems in the banking industry. However, this improvement takes on a more central role in fraud management systems due to the rapidly changing nature of fraud. Every time there is a leap forward in the digital world, there is an equal leap forward in what the fraudsters can do to increase the losses to the bank. Banks have to always stay a step ahead of the fraudsters, and they can do so by acknowledging that the cycle of improvement never ends.

SUMMARY

In this chapter, we looked at the important ingredients to developing a great fraud management DNA in the organization. This starts with a lot of simple, clean steps, all of which combine to create an awesome fraud management environment. Overlooking any of the steps affects the overall effectiveness of the system.

In the next chapter, we will specifically examine the operational aspects of a good fraud management system. The world's best technology in fraud detection is meaningless unless it is effectively integrated into the operational environment.

CHAPTER **5**

It Is Not Real Progress Until It Is Operational

When I think of operationalizing analytics for fraud management, I am reminded of this saying: "Knowledge is knowing that tomato is a fruit; wisdom is knowing not to put it in fruit salad." Knowledge of the results of a fraud model—even very thorough knowledge—does not guarantee the best results in the production use of the model. Very careful thought must go into deciding how the model will be used in production and what actions need to be taken to achieve the desired customer service and fraud control results. We can have the best data, the best methods to extract information to use in a fraud model, and the best analytical techniques to detect fraud, but if the performance metrics set for the model or the way in which the fraud score is used in production is not aligned with how business objectives are set, the fraud management system is unlikely to be very useful in managing fraud.

For fraud detection, operationalizing fraud analytics is as important as using a data-driven analytical system. Any gap in the collaboration among the operations, business, IT, and analytics teams can have undesired outcomes. This chapter will examine the specific challenges involved in operationalizing fraud solutions and how best to deal with these challenges. The teams each play a key role in this, and no single team's role is any less crucial than the roles of the other teams.

It is important for this partnership among operations, business, IT, and analytics to start early on in the project. The partnership cannot be an afterthought; it must be the driving force behind the entire project. I mention operations and business separately here even though often this is the same team. Operations in general is very heavily involved in the tactical day-to-day contacting of customers and managing the fraud queues. Business guides operations but also is involved in both the strategic and tactical aspects of fraud management. I will continue to mention operations and business separately with this in mind even though, from time to time, in certain aspects of fraud management, there is considerable overlap.

THE IMPORTANCE OF PRESENTING A SOLID PICTURE

Bill Russell, the American basketball player, played center for the Boston Celtics and is widely considered to be one of the best players in NBA history. He once said, "The idea is not to block every shot. The idea is to make your opponent believe that you might block every shot."[1] The same principle applies to fraud management. We may not be able to stop every fraudulent transaction, but we need to make sure the bank presents a very solid picture of the fraud management infrastructure to the ever-growing fraudster community so that it isn't seen as an easy target.

It is important for any financial institution to keep the fraudsters guessing what its next move against fraud might be. A fraud detection system that is predictable is not effective in combating fraud. This is one of the reasons why most rules-based systems start to lose their effectiveness as time passes. It is easy for a fraudster to figure out what rule has been implemented by using a few trials. In a data-driven high-end analytical system, though, guessing exactly how the system would react to a particular transaction is next to impossible. In addition to that, in this era of customer sophistication and increased expectations, it is important to make every customer feel that his/her legitimate transactions will not be accidentally blocked by strict fraud management measures. It is necessary to balance catching every attempted fraud with allowing every legitimate transaction, even though this balance is difficult to achieve.

In order to present a unified and secure fraud management environment to both good customers and fraudsters, it will be important for operations, business, IT, and analytics to work together with a common goal. By analytics, I am referring to teams involved in creating vendor models as well as teams involved in creating bank-developed rules, whether or not they depend on hardcore statistical techniques. Data analysis basically leads to these rules (some sophisticated and some not so sophisticated) to develop a close partnership among the teams on the project from the beginning. Apart from ensuring all parties understand and appreciate the roles of the other members, the partnership will also yield the wonderful side benefit of fulfilling the increasingly significant model governance requirements that a number of banks now have. Model governance played a significant role in monitoring and approving credit risk models a couple of decades ago and was not much involved in approving fraud risk models. The reason for this was very simple. Credit risk models affected credit line management, over-limit approval decisions, and the like, while fraud risk models were used to identify which customers were likely compromised, quickly stop the compromise, and get new card and other identities issued. A growing trend lately is that there is significant involvement of model governance teams in the fraud risk models as well. The earlier these teams are brought into the process, the smoother the approval process will be.

Also, staying involved in the project from the very beginning will give operations, business, IT, and analytics a true picture of the entire project and how the models can be used effectively in production. This environment of shared responsibility and mutual respect among the teams yields the best results. I will go one step further and say that without this partnership, it is hard to expect successful completion of a data-driven fraud management system.

BUILDING AN EFFECTIVE MODEL

Let's look at how a data-driven fraud management project is typically run. Any fraud modeling project starts with collecting historic data over a period of time. The length of data typically covers a period that is representative of the seasonality seen in fraud episodes, say a year or so. Fraud episodes vary significantly throughout the year. In order for a model suite to generalize well, it is important to have this seasonality represented in the data used to build the model. The data used to build the model suite must be detailed transaction-level data since summarized data will likely hide a number of important patterns that are essential in fraud detection.

Let's consider the following example from the credit card world. Cash withdrawals in casinos, especially at odd hours in the night, are very risky from a fraud perspective. Let's say we have a customer who withdraws a lot of cash regularly and his card has been compromised. If the information available is daily or summarized every few hours, the activity might look normal. However, looking into the details of the transactions—how often the transactions are taking place, where they are taking place, and what time the transactions are taking place—would reveal that the activity is likely perpetrated by a fraudster. Detailed transactional information is important not only for credit or debit cards but for all types of bank products because a lot of information is embedded in the transactional details. The most sophisticated fraud models use not only detailed monetary transactions but also nonmonetary, billing, and application transactions. This level of detail combined with the latest analytical techniques improves model performance dramatically.

Access to historical transactional data stored and available with the details of which transactions turned out to be fraudulent will be essential to building good fraud models. One daunting challenge in fraud model building is the censored nature of the problem. Unlike other risk problems where we are trying to predict who is likely to go delinquent or leave the bank in the future, with fraud we are trying to detect the fraud as quickly as possible during the fraud episode and stop it. Ironically, the sooner we stop the fraud problem, the less data we have for the next round of model building. Let's contrast this with credit risk.

Typically, we try to predict in advance which customer is likely to go seriously delinquent, go bankrupt, or get charged off. We would like to be able to predict this risk several months in advance. When we assemble historical data to tackle this problem, the risk phenomena and the normal transactions in the account are separated by several months. There is clean data available from the past that can be used intelligently to predict who is likely to go delinquent. In the fraud problem, since we are trying to detect fraud while it is occurring and as quickly as possible, often transactions that get stopped in their tracks don't get recorded. This means that the data available for model building the next time around is not as rich as it could have been. While the transactions that resulted in money flowing out of the customer's account are kept track of diligently, quite often, transactions that don't result in quantifiable losses (those transactions that were effectively stopped by the fraud detection system), referred to as zero monetary loss transactions, are not tracked. There is significant information in the transactions that were stopped successfully, whether it was done through the use of scores from the current model or it was done through the use of expert written rules. Keeping track of these transactions tends to be more an operations/IT function than a business or analytics function.

Keeping good track of fraud and non-fraud transactions plays a key role in the efficacy of the model suite that is built. While building the next-generation fraud model suite, if we ignore all the transactions that were successfully identified and stopped in the past, the resulting model will be much less effective in stopping fraud than the previous model. Again, effective partnership among operations, business, IT, and analytics is needed in all aspects of fraud management, from data collection all the way to measurement of model performance and use of the model scores in production.

An effective model should stop fraud that is being handled well by the current system and attempt to stop a significant portion of the fraud that is not being identified by the current system. Both are important. The constantly evolving nature of fraud demands both be addressed. As we saw in earlier chapters, fraud is no longer an opportunistic phenomenon. It is perpetrated very systematically by organized crime rings. The methods of fraud are evolving fast, and this requires fraud detection systems constantly to evolve and become more sophisticated.

Sometimes this begins with the simplest details, like saving up all the bits of information associated with the fraud episode.

We will consider model performance measurement in detail in the coming chapters. Model performance measurement is not only for PhDs and analytics folks. The measurement of the model should be aligned with how the model will be used in production. Hence, a broad understanding of what the model is attempting to detect is very important for the fraud analysts in operations, IT, and the analytics teams. If the model is fine-tuned to detect monetary losses and the operations are aligned to detect compromised entities, the best results cannot be achieved. The objectives of the multiple teams must be aligned in order to achieve the best results. We will look at the importance of fraud measurement in later chapters.

In this chapter, let's specifically discuss the challenges in operationalizing fraud models. The challenges in operationalizing fraud models fall broadly into four categories:

1. Operations personnel need to understand the concept of a *fraud score*.
2. The score development process must take into consideration operational use and constraints.
3. In general, fraud strategies should complement and not compete with the fraud score.
4. Fraud strategies and operational processes should be well documented.

Let's examine each one of these challenges in detail.

1. Operations Personnel Need to Understand the Concept of a *Fraud Score*

The term *scoring* started as a way to keep track of outcomes in a systematic manner. For example, if you are at a basketball game and a score is kept, it is simply a record of what happened during the game. Assuming the referee's words are final, there is not much guesswork in the score and it is simply a record of the past. However, for scoring in risk management, the score typically represents the outcome of a statistical model that examines the transactions and estimates the likelihood of serious risk in the future (in the case of credit risk) or serious transition to risk right now (as in the case of fraud risk). Also, if we look at fraud scoring, because the phenomenon of fraud is rare, even an excellent score will likely have a number of misses—namely legitimate accounts that get a high (risky) score. Let's examine the numbers behind this.

Fraud, as ubiquitous as it seems, occurs very infrequently. Card fraud runs less than ten basis points in a number of portfolios. A basis point (BP) is a unit equal to 1/100 of 1 percent and so ten basis points is 1/10 of 1 percent. Basis points in fraud assumes that fraud is measured in monetary losses. While the BP measurements are typically used against actual monetary loss, the monetary loss may not be uniformly distributed across transactions.

For the sake of simplicity, let's assume that fraud is measured at a transaction level and roughly 1 in 1,000 transactions is fraudulent. In order to decide whether to take action on a particular transaction or not, let's say we relied on flipping a coin instead of a score. Let's also assume that it is a biased coin and the likelihood of fraud is represented by the heads of the coin.

If the outcome of the coin flipping determines how we will treat the transaction with respect to fraud, we are not likely to do any better than the underlying fraud probability (1 in 1,000 in this example). In other words, by flipping this biased coin, in any set of transactions we identify as fraudulent, 1 in 1,000 will turn out to be fraudulent. We will not be doing any better than random chance. When we use a score, we are relying on the score to determine whether to take action on a transaction or not. We would like the score to increase our chances of identifying fraud to be much higher than the underlying probability of fraud. In other words, if we can identify a population of transactions using a score that increases the likelihood of fraud to 1 in 100 from 1 in 1,000 and if we can get a significant concentration of fraud (say more than 50 percent of the overall fraud) in this population, we are doing much better than flipping a biased coin. Better yet, if we can identify a population of transactions where there is a 1-in-20 chance of finding fraud and the concentration of fraud is significant and the concentration of non-frauds is insignificant, we are doing phenomenally well. We have reduced the fraud problem that is a 1-in-1,000 problem to a problem that is 1-in-20 while making sure there is enough percentage of the overall fraud in the group. It is important to have enough fraud in the group of transactions identified. For example, it is possible to write a great rule that identifies a very small group of transactions with a heavy concentration of frauds. However, if the number of frauds in the group is a minuscule percentage of the overall population of frauds, the fraud problem will persist even though this one rule has excellent results. So, to tackle the fraud problem, we need to focus on identifying a set of transactions rich in fraud, and our set of transactions needs to be big enough to matter.

Let's look at the scenario we started with. Let's say fraud is occurring in 1 in 1,000 transactions and we have a score that can identify a large enough group of transactions that has a 1-in-20 concentration of fraud. Basically, if we contact every customer in the group to verify their transactions, 1 contact in every 20 contacts will yield the desired result of catching or correctly identifying fraud. When we look at the overall fraud problem, this seems like a very good improvement. However, looking at it from an operations point of view, having to make 20 calls to identify a single fraud is a laborious and tedious task. If, by chance, an analyst figures out a subjective way to identify fraud in a very small group of transactions and if the analyst starts relying on this method instead of calling the accounts qualified by the scoring system in the queue, the results will be counterproductive.

In order to avoid this subjectivity issue, it is very important to educate the fraud operations analysts how rare the fraud problem is and what the analytics-based scoring system is attempting to do. Also, it is very important to help the operations staff see the forest from the trees. Working the individual queues where most of the calls to customers reveal legitimate transactions might make the analysts think that the system is not effective. Unless there is effective training on how rare the fraud problem is and how much improvement is achieved using a scoring system, the score-based queues will not be utilized as they are intended. The ultimate effectiveness of a fraud detection system is very much dependent on how well the queues are managed by the analysts. Regardless of how superior the fraud scores are, what matters ultimately is how well the analysts handled the queues. Many fraud departments are still unaware of the importance of this crucial component.

Training the analysts is important also because transaction activity is growing in leaps and bounds and in a lot of the new channels, like mobile fraud, events are even rarer than what we have seen in the more traditional channels such as point of sale (POS). Even though the instance of fraud is very rare in these new channels, the cost to the bank of a single episode can be huge. Automated clearing house (ACH) and wire transactions are a great example of this. Fraud episodes in these transactions can be up to 100 times rarer than card and other fraud. However, each instance of fraud can cost the bank dearly. A single episode of ACH or wire fraud can run in the hundreds of thousands of dollars. In cases like this, it becomes extremely important to follow what the sophisticated analytics-based system is recommending. Second-guessing the data-driven, analytics-based system should be monitored and curbed effectively.

One of the most surprising things to me in the area of fraud detection is how compartmentalized the knowledge can be. While it is not realistic to expect the same level of knowledge of scores to exist in the operations team as we see among members of the analytics team, sometimes even a basic level of knowledge doesn't exist. A deeper understanding of the meaning of scores will certainly result in better use of the scores by the analysts. Whenever I get a call from the fraud detection department of my credit card company, I quiz them on what my fraud score is. When they quote a number, I ask them what the number means, feigning ignorance on my part. The answer I usually get clearly tells me that there is serious lack of knowledge in the operations area on what these scores mean and why they should be used. Improving the appreciation of scoring and why it is essential can have an extremely positive impact on the operational use of analytics-based systems. When I make this recommendation, I fully realize that this will not be an easy educational process as the skill sets of operations personnel and analytics teams are fundamentally different. With the common goal of effective fraud management in mind, I think this can be achieved if enough effort is put into training. While trying to demystify a score and explain how a score is X for a particular transaction can be difficult to do, some fundamental knowledge of what a score is attempting to do (reduce a 1-in-1,000 problem to a 1-in-20 problem) will go a long way in ensuring there is no slip between the cup and the lip.

2. The Score Development Process Must Take into Consideration Operational Use and Constraints

Switching gears to how the scores are developed and what aspects of score development can be improved, I cannot stress enough the importance of understanding operational processes thoroughly in the development of analytics-based scores. When a fraud model suite is developed, it is literally impossible to build a model with absolutely uniform performance across all types of fraud and across all types of portfolios. The fraud model performance to be achieved in these different segments must be aligned with how the scores are used in production.

Let's take a couple of examples. In general, every portfolio has a premier customer population. These are customers the bank doesn't want to bother very often to verify transactions. Let's say that the normal annoyance level at which queues are worked is 20:1. However, for this population, the annoyance level needs to be much lower, say 5:1. Let's say the portfolio that the model is designed for has 50 percent premier accounts. Let's say the model is tuned to do very well at 20:1. Typically, if a model is tuned to do well at 20:1, the model does well at lower annoyance levels as well. Let's pretend for the sake of this example that the model does way better at 20:1 than it does at 5:1. If the fact that the acceptable annoyance level for premier customers should be 5:1 is not considered in model building or in model performance measurement, the results in production will be far inferior. Knowledge of operations is very important to building effective analytic models.

Let's consider a different example. There are many different kinds of fraud that have to be handled by any fraud detection system. Sometimes fraud starts with a fraudulent application. With this account, most of the transactions are fraud, but it takes a lot of skill to identify and close the account as fraudulent before the perpetrator decides to abandon the account. This becomes tricky as the perpetrator is the one who gets the call from the bank, and he/she will confirm the transactions as legitimate. The analysts who deal effectively with this type of fraud are highly sought after and hence more expensive in terms of compensation. The false positive ratio the bank is willing to tolerate on this type of fraud is very low, and hence the models need to be very good at this particular detection. There is the lost-and-stolen fraud where a card was lost at a store and a person who gets the card decides to opportunistically charge a few transactions to it. In this fraud, it is a relatively simple exercise to contact the cardholder and confirm the transaction as fraud. A smile-and-dial analyst might do a very good job of confirming fraud in such a case. With the proliferation of Internet merchants, card-not-present fraud has taken on a life of its own. As recently as ten years ago, card-not-present fraud used to be under 10 percent of the overall fraud. Now it runs anywhere from 30 percent to 60 percent of the overall fraud in most portfolios. This type of fraud is complex from two different points of view.

First, new Internet merchants get created and eliminated overnight. It becomes challenging to learn about these merchants if our learning process depended on long history as there is no such history available. While there are many Internet merchants with lengthy history, there are a lot with very little history. Even the Internet merchants with lengthy history keep changing in terms of volume with the introduction of new sales and new merchandise offerings. The rate of change among Internet merchants seems to be much higher than brick-and-mortar retail merchants.

And second, card-not-present fraud is perhaps the one fraud type where not all of the fraud liability falls on the bank. In fact, most often the liability falls on the merchants. However, from time to time, liability shifts between the issuing bank and the Internet merchant. This makes the problem challenging from the modeling and operations perspectives. If the model assumes all of card-not-present fraud is not the issuing bank's problem and deemphasizes this type of fraud, a shift in liability could lead to a significant increase in the fraud losses for the bank. If the model assumes that card-not-present fraud is as important as any other type of fraud, it may not yield the type of dollar detection performance that we need from the model. A balancing act is necessary to make sure the model considers this type of fraud but does not over- or underemphasize it.

The examples given above do not exhaustively cover all the operational considerations to be used in effective model building. Apart from type of customer, fraud type, and so on, a number of issues, such as the volume that operations can handle on a daily basis, the true business goals of the bank (for example, whether to reduce fraud or reduce customer annoyance), holiday period considerations, segments of customers that need to be considered for top-level segmentation of the models, and model score alignment need to be considered very carefully during the model-building process. In order for the model to become the driving force in operations once it is implemented, understanding all the operational constraints and using them during the model-building process are essential.

A word about model score calibration. To put it in simple terms, the output of a model is turned into a number that refers to the score cut-off that identifies fraud. It is very important for this number to be aligned so it's very easy to change models and still use the majority of the operational fraud strategies. This again is an operational consideration that sometimes gets overlooked during model building. From a pure model perspective, the alignment does not have any impact on model performance. However, from an operations perspective and ease of use, correct alignment of the models makes a world of difference. There needs to be discussion of how the model gets calibrated for ease of use in production. This ease of use should be one of the main criteria driving calibrations of successive generations of models as well.

Apart from what we discussed already in this section, the teams need to consider very carefully all the fields used in the model to make sure the use of these fields is allowed and that using these fields makes sense for the purpose of fraud management. This requires understanding why some of the variables created are good indicators of fraud. It is important to ensure that correlation is not being incorrectly interpreted as a causal relationship between the outcome and the variables. This will ensure that the model is valid and robust in production over a long period of time. To accomplish this, there needs to be close collaboration between the domain experts in the bank and the vendors who develop the fraud detection systems.

The importance of expert input into building a data-driven model cannot be overemphasized. Data mining in a vacuum might yield interesting results but without the context of expert input, these results don't mean a lot. In fraud detection, as regulatory scrutiny is less than what we see in the area of credit risk, there is a tendency to blindly follow what the data says. Data mining used in conjunction with expert input will deliver wonderful results.

3. In General, Fraud Strategies Should Complement and Not Compete with the Fraud Score

In the previous section, we discussed in detail the importance of developing the model suite, taking into consideration all operational processes and constraints. Once such a model is developed, we should rely on it consistently and make decisions based on it. What we find in most operational environments, though, is that even after an excellent model suite is developed, there is heavy reliance on rules that have effectively been made unimportant by the model. This is like buying an electric saw that works wonders and then instead of using it, continuing to use a hand saw, and then wondering in the end why we are unable to achieve better results. There are a few different reasons for this.

Rules are easy to understand. Since rules make intuitive sense, they appeal to operations staff from a usage perspective also. There is no systematic measurement of rules and how effective they are at stopping fraud in the presence of other rules. Since there is no established process of measuring rules individually and as a group, it is easy to miss the fact that they are ineffective in the presence of the new model. So their usage continues. One might ask why this is a bad thing.

As in a lot of production processes, fraud management from an operations perspective is a constrained process, constrained by resources. There are only so many hours in a day and there are only so many fraud analysts managing fraud queues. Even with the use of automated predictive dialers, there is a limit to the volume of calls that can be handled in a given period of time. The time-sensitive nature of fraud is a major concern, too. Typical fraud windows only run for a few hours with the longest ones (except in the case of fraudulent applications) running only for a few days. If, during this limited period of time, we do not interrupt the fraud episode and stop it, the fraud episode is done and there is nothing that can be done to impact the losses. With this context in mind, it becomes clear very quickly that the opportunity cost of not using a good fraud model to stop fraud and instead using rules that are not as effective is huge. For some reason, this fact is totally lost on many operations departments in banks.

It is a very straightforward exercise to create a business case for a sophisticated fraud detection system. One simple way to do this is as follows: There is a daily quota of fraud cases that can be handled by the operations staff in any bank. Among these cases, there is a certain number that turn out to be fraud. These represent the fraud savings and the benefit side of the equation; cases that don't turn out to be fraud are good customers who get verification calls (or what we call "false positives"). This broadly represents the cost side of the equation. If the same number of cases is allowed for a new system and if the new system can better identify fraud, while the benefit side of the equation becomes better, simultaneously the cost side of the equation gets better as well since there are a fixed number of cases. To give a specific example, let's say an operations department can handle 1000 cases in a day and among the 1,000 cases identified by a simple rules-based system, there are 25 fraud cases (representing a false positive ratio of 40:1). If a model-based system can identify 100 fraud cases among the 1,000 cases that the system chooses, not only does the benefit of identifying true fraud go up from 25 cases to 100, the number of false positives simultaneously is reduced from 975 to 900. It becomes a straightforward exercise to build a business case by looking at the average benefit of stopping a fraud episode and the average cost of annoying a good customer. There is additional value that can be derived when considering the effect of more than just 1,000 cases. All that becomes icing on the cake.

A classic example of the ineffectiveness of the operational use of an advanced scoring system is how the use of scores is abruptly stopped beyond a certain false positive ratio. The use of scores to determine the cases to queue is very common in scores referring to low false positive rates. However, once the false positive ratios go higher than 20:1, the use of scores effectively ends. A good score is a wonderful rank-ordering tool and hence usable even in the low-scoring range, not just in the high-scoring range. If there is capacity available in the queues beyond 20:1, the logical process to follow would be to use the score in the lower range as well. Even in cases where we are trying to cherry pick fraud in the low-scoring regions using some highly specialized rules, it would make sense to use the score as one of the criteria to eliminate the obvious non-fraud cases. The score is meant to the represent the sum total of the knowledge that can be gleaned from the associated data. Hence, the score is usable in all ranges, not just the high-scoring range.

In operations, it is essential to develop the mind-set of complementing the score (and using it as much as possible) and not competing with the score. As mentioned earlier, this starts with training the operations department on the importance of the score, continued review of all processes to ensure the score is being used to its full potential, and continued ongoing monitoring of all the strategies to assess efficacy individually and with the rule as a member of the set of strategies. The process of education should start at the very beginning of the project so that operations staff have the opportunity early on to learn about the model(s) and why using the model(s) will lead to superior results.

In operations, some strategies need to be created for specific operational reasons, such as information just received on a fraud outbreak in a particular zip code. In such cases, it makes sense to ignore the score and take action according to what the operational need is. This, however, should be used as an exception sparingly. When a new model suite is developed and released, it is important to completely rethink fraud strategies and examine every one of them to make sure the strategy is adding value to the overall fraud management process. Systematic examination and measurement of fraud strategies requires a reporting system that is tied to the operations. This reporting system should run on a data warehouse that stores all the data flowing through the fraud management solution and keeps track of the scores and reason codes produced, the strategies that were used against the transactions, and the outcome of using these strategies. Strategies are simply the logic that is used in production to use scores in conjunction with other decision keys to decide what to do with a particular transaction. Some of the strategies may not rely on scores at all and can simply be based on what the domain experts choose to do operationally.

A reporting systems that keeps track of scores, reason codes, and strategies not only produces valuable information on the ongoing performance of the fraud strategies (as well as scores); it can also monitor the data flowing through the system and look for any drastic data changes. The same system can be used to test new fraud strategies written against a data repository that is representative of production data. Having this single version of the truth in terms of fraud management data can be extremely useful in the upkeep of the system.

Considering the evolving sophistication of the fraudster community, identifying the common point of purchase that caused a compromise can throw a lot of light on which customers should be advised of possible compromise even before fraud starts on their accounts. For this, a reliable source of past information is essential. Once a data warehouse is established and linked to the fraud management system, a number of uses can be derived from it. The same warehouse can also be used to monitor the fraud models regularly, and any degradation in model performance or change in fraud patterns in the portfolio can be identified and addressed effectively in a timely manner.

4. Fraud Strategies and Operational Processes Should Be Well Documented

Once a good score and an appropriate set of fraud strategies are developed, the job is not done. The actual handling of the cases in production is not done by the personnel who develop the scores or the strategies. Let's take the example of a fraudulent application. We saw earlier that this type of fraud is hard to stop as the perpetrator is also the account holder. When the fraud analyst calls the customer to verify if a transaction was fraudulent, unlike in other cases of fraud, the customer is going to confirm the transaction was legitimate. In this case, the call must be handled with finesse, and it is not simply to verify the transaction. The goal is to extract more information from the perpetrator. There are sophisticated scoring solutions that not only give a score indicative of fraud but can also pinpoint and predict the type of fraud that is being perpetrated. With or without such solutions, it will be important to train the fraud analysts to treat fraud cases appropriately. To achieve uniformity in terms of effectiveness, the best strategy is to clearly and thoroughly document the processes used by the analysts. This takes the guesswork out of how the fraud queues are handled in production.

In addition to documenting the analysts' work, it is important to document fraud strategies carefully as well. There have been many occasions when emergencies occur in bank fraud operations because of a fraud strategy that was not thoroughly tested and documented. Documenting the strategies also helps all concerned parties to understand the strategies. If a strategy needs to be modified in the future, it will be easier to do that if the original intent of the strategy is clearly understood.

The documentation of the strategies and periodic performance reports (as mentioned in the previous section) will lead to better use of the fraud strategies.

SUMMARY

The four challenges discussed in this chapter, when addressed well, will lead to real progress in operations. Regardless of how sophisticated the systems are, unless all the components of fraud management are run well, the expected results just will not flow in. The law of averages doesn't work very well in this case. There is a saying that a statistician is one who has one hand in ice and one hand in fire and says on the average he is OK. This averaging approach does not work in fraud management. We cannot have an amazing model but suboptimal operations and say we will be OK on the average. By the same token, we cannot have amazingly well-run operations but a poor fraud detection model and expect to do very well. It is important to get all aspects of fraud management right. No single aspect of fraud management should be totally or even marginally ignored. It is important to have a well-thought-out fraud model that understands operational constraints, an operational setup that utilizes the full potential of the model, a set of well-developed strategies that utilize the model score as well as domain expert's knowledge, and an operational process that is thoroughly documented and understood by everyone involved in the execution of the process.

Another interesting aspect of operationalizing analytics is the role of authentication versus detection. Roughly a decade ago, as I mentioned earlier in the book, I was invited by one of the credit card associations to be on a panel to discuss the roles of authentication and detection in fraud management. To make the terminology clear: *Authentication* is the process of ascertaining a customer's identity positively while he/she is attempting a transaction. The goal in authentication is zero ambiguity. A good example of authentication is when the bank provides a personal identification number (PIN) that the customer enters to positively identify the person attempting the transaction. In *detection*, what we try to do is identify the customer using more indirect ways. Let's say I have never withdrawn cash in a casino. A model can use that information to decide whether this cash withdrawal was initiated by me or a fraudster. Detection cannot always be foolproof, because when a customer attempts a particular type of transaction that he or she has never initiated in the past, it will most likely look suspect from a detection or model-driven system perspective. Contrast this with authentication where some specific pieces of information are verified to positively identify the customer. Thus, authentication has enjoyed the respect of the fraud management community. In the fraud panel, some of my fellow experts believed that due to the evolving complexities of detecting fraud, authentication methods would become more and more popular and detection would become almost obsolete.

What actually happened in the decade since is somewhat the opposite of those predictions. Ever-increasing complexities with computers, IP addresses, networks, and sophisticated cyber-attacks have rendered simple authentication methods no longer foolproof. Before accepting a PIN as being valid, for example, now it is essential to ascertain if the IP address is consistent with what the institution has seen for this customer. When there are large-scale data thefts, all of the information provided for authentication can be valid and correct but it is still possible that the person transacting is a fraudster. For example, if a customer has never transacted from Russia and we see that the latest request from this customer has a Russian IP address associated with it, it becomes essential to validate whether the customer is who he/she is claiming to be, even if the PIN and several other authentication criteria match exactly. Clearly, there is a movement toward behavioral observations and detection-like methods to confirm the identity of the customer. Contrary to what was predicted, authentication also needs to rely on analytical techniques to confirm identity. This opens up a world of possibilities.

Data never before available to fraud detection systems on the customer's activity is now available in the digital world through authentication systems. This data can be combined with previously collected data to have significant impact on the overall fraud picture. On the authentication side, sophisticated systems can track use of devices across multiple banks. If a POS transaction is preceded by a fraudster checking the validity of the card on the Internet, that information can be used to further combat fraud. A significant amount of data can be collected on the authentication side of the equation as well in such cases. I predict that systems that bring authentication and authorization systems closer together will help define the future of fraud management.

Next, we will examine why in the case of fraud management, all the aspects we have discussed are almost equally important. Current fraud management depends on all aspects of the process running smoothly, and the future of fraud management at an institution depends on how well the process is run today. We will see why this chain is only as strong as its weakest link in the next chapter.

CHAPTER **6**

The Chain Is Only as Strong as Its Weakest Link

Supply chain management uses the mantra "The chain is only as strong as its weakest link." In any area, when a game-changing technology is introduced, there tends to be an overreliance on the technology while other very important aspects of the overall process are ignored. The devil in this case is in the details. Supply chain management is more like a relay race where each participant has to effectively complete his/her segment of the race or else the race is lost. This analogy applies well to fraud management. Even with the best technology, if certain fundamental principles are not adhered to, good results cannot be expected. It is important for these fundamental principles to be followed by everyone involved in the chain, not just a few.

In this chapter, we will dive deeper to understand the essential steps involved in building a model. The purpose of this chapter is not to convert the reader into a data science/modeling expert (which requires considerable academic training and practice). The purpose is to give enough understanding of the steps involved so that members of the extended team of operations, business, IT, and analytics discussed in the previous chapter can gain an appreciation of what is involved and the important contributions they will be making to the overall process.

DISTINCT STAGES OF A DATA-DRIVEN FRAUD MANAGEMENT SYSTEM

In order to understand why this is the case, let's begin by seeing how a data-driven fraud management system works and the stages in the process. Please note that there are other possible ways to look at this. What I have described below covers the major components of the process, but there are several ways to define the stages.

The seven distinct stages, as shown in Figure 6.1, are:

1. Gather data
2. Clean and analyze data
3. Design and build model
4. Package and test model

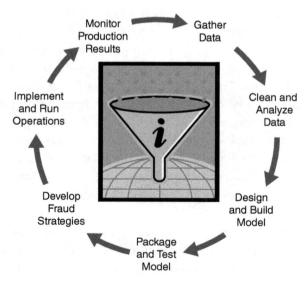

Figure 6.1 Major Components of the Data-Driven Fraud Management System

5. Develop fraud strategies

6. Implement and run operations

7. Monitor production results

The last stage in the cycle, "monitor production results," leads us right back to stage #1, "gather data." Gathering data is fundamental to any data-driven system. We touched upon gathering data briefly in the previous chapter.

Most of the stages don't involve high-end technology. A significant step in gathering the right data begins with defining and storing data appropriately. Some of the common issues are inadequate definition of the data field being gathered, lack of integrity of the data field, and/or not enough history of the data field being stored. A culture of "every piece of data is sacrosanct" has to be in place. Notice that this doesn't involve the PhDs in a bank. Often it is the person in IT who is the keeper of the data and definitions who needs to realize the importance of every piece of information. Many a sophisticated model has been derailed by one or two data fields changing midstream in production. Models are typically built based on the data distributions, and when the distributions change (due to changes), the model efficacy takes a dip as well.

Let's say we have defined a segment in production based on time-since-first-activity—a simple calculation. Take today's date and subtract the first day when there was activity on the account. Typically, the sourcing of the account has a major impact on when exactly transactions begin. In a number of cases where there is low credit risk and the account was booked by the bank soliciting it, activity may not start on the account immediately. However, if the customer applied and got the line of credit or credit card (or whatever product), activity is likely to start on the account right away. Segmentation based on this could delineate risk quite well. Let's say the field that indicates first activity date for some reason got changed to the open date of the account. All of a sudden, this seemingly innocent change in data field could have a significant impact on risk models.

This is a good example of why every change in data needs to have an approval process and needs to be managed very carefully. Unfortunately, this cardinal rule is rarely followed. There has to be a whole culture of reviewing and treating any data field change with a great amount of care and respect. This begins with education and establishing a close-knit culture of monitoring change carefully.

THE ESSENTIALS OF BUILDING A GOOD FRAUD MODEL

Once we go from gathering data to cleaning and analyzing data, the task becomes one of understanding the past issues in data and documenting them so that if questions come up, there is a clear trail of what has been done. A good fraud model relies heavily on learning from past fraud episodes. There are unsupervised modeling techniques that can handle types of fraud with no fraud history captured (observing and analyzing anomalies in the data), but if fraud data is available, the models including the historical data are bound to be better. Learning from real fraud examples in the past is far superior to simply observing anomalies in the data. Unsupervised models are more useful for frauds such as automated clearing house (ACH) and wire fraud, network intrusion, and internal fraud, where very few known cases of that type of fraud exist. Being able to clearly differentiate which declined transactions happened because of fraud and which declined transactions were for other reasons is essential to building a good fraud model.

In addition to target or fraud data, when analyzing data from the past, explanations for missing data need to be available so that the missing data can be understood in context. With clean data, the quality of the models and the fraud strategies will improve dramatically. In today's systems where a dedicated fraud management data warehouse stores all the data that was utilized by the fraud management system—including scores and reason codes—the successive generations of models are significantly better than the previous versions, simply due to access to better data.

Consortium-Based Models

In the previous chapter, we discussed, in some detail, the need for designing the model that is aligned with operations. While building the model, especially if this is a fraud model built by a vendor, very little knowledge sharing is done. There could be significant operational and business considerations that are completely missed by the vendor if the model-building process doesn't involve an active exchange of ideas. Vendors are not in the business of teaching banks how to build their own fraud models if that is the vendors' core competency. However, this doesn't mean that vendors build fraud models in isolation and just throws models over the wall for the banks to use either. The topic of consortium-based models is relevant to this discussion. A fraud consortium is where a number of banks contribute data to a vendor and the vendor builds a consortium data-based model and ships the model to most if not all the banks. Historically two decades ago this was a decent approach as there were many small banks and there was benefit to be had by combining data. The downfall of this approach is that every bank is forced to use data that is the least common denominator of the data that is available across all issuers. In other words, the chain again is only as strong as its weakest link. Being able to produce a single model and market it to all banks is certainly a great strategy and lot less work for the vendor. However, this is not the optimal solution for the banks, considering the rapid consolidation that has happened in the marketplace in the last tenyears or so. Even with the smaller banks, if they have some unique data assets by way of unique data fields (compromise data and such), there is a lot of benefit to using all this data—the data that is likely to be dropped if a consortium model approach is used.

The good news is that there are sophisticated techniques available now that utilize the best of both worlds. Banks can still continue to contribute to a consortium to get the benefit of the fraud trends observed in the entire industry while utilizing their unique data assets as well. There are ways to introduce mini models into the fraud model suite by way of variables that capture fraud trends from the industry and also utilize the uniqueness of the data in individual own portfolios.

Deciding If the Juice Is Worth the Squeeze

One of the people in the San Diego analytics community that I have learned a lot from is Lynn Wallis, and he is not even a scientist by training. As both my manager and my mentor, he has had a profound influence on my understanding of the business significance of analytics. He is known for his pithy one-sentence quotes, and one of the really popular ones is "Is the juice worth the squeeze?" I know this has been used by a lot of people, but it is very relevant to fraud detection models.

As the models become more sophisticated, ensuring that they will work the same way in the production environment as they did in the modeling environment is an important stage in the overall process. The model package must not only produce expected results from an analytics perspective, but also the system resources it consumes need to be in line with the value it adds. I read somewhere that success and how far one succeeds in life should be measured by what that person had to give up in life to achieve the success. This is true of any risk management system, too. We need to ask ourselves whether the juice is worth the squeeze. Let's say we have a perfect fraud model that can completely identify all the fraud occurring in a portfolio. However, if the model takes so long to run in production that it crashes the production system, that model is far from desirable. Also, if the model ends up annoying a huge proportion of the customers in order to stop fraud, it will not be very useful.

In this context, I am reminded of a funny incident from when I was 11 years old. I come from a very humble background, and our family had just completed building a modest house in the suburbs of Chennai. The flooring was not laid yet and I heard repeated discussions at the dinner table about how we should have a classy floor in the living room to lift the look of the entire house. There were discussions about what would be the best material to use on the floor. As an ignorant 11-year-old, I had no idea about the cost of things. When these discussions were going on, a brand-new cinema that was the best in the entire area opened in town. My parents, my brother, and I went to see a movie there, and I totally fell in love with the marble floor and walls in the theater. It was a beautiful brick red with grey and black specks and also some hints of a silver and gold shine. It was just beautiful.

I got very excited. I came home and during dinner that night, I told my mom and dad that I had the perfect suggestion for the living room floor. I went on to say, "Dad! Did you see the beautiful marble floor and walls at Brinda Theater? I think that would be perfect for our house living room floor." My father is one of the hardest-working people I know, and he has always had a tremendous sense of humor. He had a very easy way about him that made me feel like he was as much my friend as my father. He paused for a minute and said, "Sure, Revathi! We can do that. However, we may have to sell the house in order to afford the marble floor." Everyone burst out laughing. I had no clue what the price of the marble flooring was compared to the house. I am not sure the floor would have been as expensive as the house, but the point that my dad drove home was a very good one— we should seek out simple, elegant solutions for problems, and the solution to the problem shouldn't cost more than what the problem would cost us.

I was drawn to statistics due to the large-scale, consistent solutions that can be created for problems using statistical models so that the effort to solve the problem is much smaller than the problem itself. In a lot of ways, my dad's comment that day has shaped my subject of study and career interest. This same theme applies to the usability of the model as well.

The practical usability of the model in a high-throughput environment is as important as the fraud detection performance of the model. Similarly, one has to look at the customer annoyance factor in deciding whether stopping the fraud losses make sense. One foolproof way to stop fraud is to stop all transactions, examine them, and then allow the legitimate ones. This method is not practical. Like a lot of things in life, it is crucial to achieve the right balance in terms of risk versus reward. This equation needs to be closely aligned with the overall business objectives and should have buy-in from all parties concerned.

Monitoring and Fine-Tuning

Tackling fraud in today's world starts with building or buying a model suite that is embedded in a fraud detection system. Once we have the fraud model ready, all existing fraud strategies need to be carefully evaluated against the new model to see if these strategies are truly bringing incremental value. Quite often, even if a fraud strategy is not necessary or is too expensive to run in production, there is no analysis done to estimate the cost of running the strategy; most of these strategies are written by domain experts, and there is significant emotional attachment to them even after there is clear evidence that the strategies have been rendered ineffective by the latest round of model building. It is crucial to have clear procedures in place to ensure that every strategy moved into production provides the desired incremental value over the score and also has enough support (meaning that there will be a decent number of customers who will qualify under the strategy and the false-positive ratio and the detection rate of the strategy are significant). The evaluation of these strategies needs to be based on fraud loss avoidance and reduction in customer annoyance, striking the right balance that aligns with the particular institution's business goals.

Fraud strategy development is ripe for innovation in monitoring and fine-tuning. Luckily, systems are beginning to be introduced in the marketplace that are capable of automatically monitoring fraud strategies and optimizing them to suggest what cutoff values should be used for the decision keys. Such systems are going to revolutionize and change rule (strategy) management.

Implementing the Model Suite

We looked at the operations associated with a fraud management system in detail in the previous chapter. Implementing the model suite and the fraud strategies involves cooperation among the business, IT, operations, and analytics teams. Fraud strategy implementation is especially important as the strategies tend to change often in production, and any weakness in this process can lead to disastrous results. Fraudsters have become increasingly sophisticated in identifying weaknesses in fraud control and utilizing them swiftly to their benefit. There are many known cases of fraudsters exploiting vulnerabilities in fraud control systems, resulting in millions of dollars in losses.

Once the models and strategies have been implemented in production, the entire process, including accumulation of data, needs to be monitored in production. This is necessary for the production process to run smoothly and to provide the right input into the next-generation model rebuild. Automating the monitoring of the models already deployed in production is also essential to ensure there is no degradation in the models. If this is an offline, one-off process, the upkeep of the fraud detection system will suffer. In today's world of constant fast-evolving fraud, it is crucial not to lose any time in the ongoing monitoring of models. While sophistication in fraud models has been progressing steadily over the last two decades, automating the monitoring of the models has not made much progress until recently. Only now are systems that include end-to-end monitoring being introduced in the marketplace. This lag has meant significant lost opportunity in fraud management. It will be crucial that financial institutions carefully consider monitoring-related features when choosing a fraud detection solution.

A GOOD FRAUD MANAGEMENT SYSTEM BEGINS WITH THE RIGHT ATTITUDE

As you can see, fraud management is a cyclical process, and it also requires tremendous commitment and cooperation from personnel in a number of different areas for the system to run effectively. I would like to challenge the reader to think of one stage in the seven stages listed above that can be totally ignored while still getting great fraud management results. It really is crystal clear that every stage of a data-driven fraud management system is extremely important and none of these stages can be ignored if we hope for stellar results.

I would argue that a good fraud management system, as with all things in life, begins with the right attitude. The right attitude in fraud management begins by educating everyone involved. The entire organization needs to be taught that all the teams involved are interconnected, and everything affects everything. Fraud can be tackled only by a partnership across the entire organization. The message that fraud is everyone's enemy and every single team member can help needs to be conveyed and reconveyed to all parties involved. There has to be shared responsibility and pride in tacking fraud.

A false impression is that only PhDs have a meaningful role to play in fraud management. This couldn't be further from the truth. Any data-centric system begins with the data. The most sophisticated analytical techniques are utterly useless if the underlying data has issues. Every single person involved in the process has an equally important role to play. From the frontline employees who talk to the customers and execute the strategies, to the back-end data analysts who ensure that all the data and changes are recorded on a regular basis to the domain, to the analytical experts who write the fraud strategies, to the executives who sponsor and oversee the project—all of these constituents are very important. If there are any differences in the importance of these participants to the overall project, they are only slight. All of these people have to peacefully coexist, help design the different portions of the project, and come together to execute the project in order for fraud management to succeed.

This process is a great example of a bottom-up as well as a top-down initiative. In a typical top-down initiative, the big picture emerges first and then the details get worked out. In a typical bottom-up initiative, smaller systems are pieced together to build larger systems; the original systems become parts of the new system. One can argue this both ways. Without a grand vision of how a data-driven fraud management system is designed (especially in today's world when enterprise fraud detection systems are being considered by many of the biggest banks, and smaller ones, too), it is literally impossible to make such a system a reality. However, if you examine the different stages of this process as listed in this chapter, it is very clear that the system needs to emerge from smaller systems and processes and that some of these systems and processes can be excellent building blocks for the new system. An enterprise fraud detection system needs to take into consideration risk across all products, but it is equally important to make sure that the enterprise system can be applicable to the individual products where fraud is truly managed. The translation layer that takes the enterprise-level prediction and converts it into how relevant the prediction is at the individual product level is crucial to any enterprise system.

The top-down and bottom-up perspectives also apply from a personnel point of view. Some portions of building this system will be effectively driven by senior management while other portions clearly rely on people involved in the details driving them. As enterprise risk management becomes a reality, it is clear that both approaches play a huge role. An enterprise system cannot be built by bringing together a number of point risk solutions. However, we also have to find a way to get use out of existing point solutions that the banks have heavily invested in, as such a rip-and-replace policy may not be feasible. The good news is that some of the most sophisticated enterprise risk management solutions can augment or, if needed, replace existing point solutions while at the same time fulfilling the promise of bringing together data from the entire enterprise to one system to get a complete picture of the customers. The ability to look at data across multiple products while being able to interpret it and evaluate it at the individual product level is a key feature of effective enterprise risk management systems.

SUMMARY

We live in exciting times. The next decade will see never-before-witnessed sophistication in data accumulation and analytics capabilities. Data privacy issues notwithstanding, the dream of being able to assess all aspects of the risk of a customer involved in a transaction by, say, looking at the transaction detail of what items the customer ordered at a restaurant and evaluating that new detail in different key contexts is not far off. In the race to use data most effectively that is just beginning, those with data handling and data analysis sophistication will come out ahead. Systems that use information from the past to forecast the future will fare far better than systems that simply recognize what happened in the past. The word *analytics* is used loosely to describe any reporting/data analysis these days. While looking at the past and learning from it is an essential step in building a predictive system, if the process just stops at that, it will be like seeing only things in the rearview mirror. Learning from the past should be used to make effective predictions about the future. The ability to make these predictions in a timely manner will determine success.

CHAPTER 7

Fraud Analytics: We Are Just Scratching the Surface

I have alluded to *fraud analytics* a number of times in the book without explaining in any detail what exactly I mean. In this chapter, we will examine the origin and evolution of predictive (or detection) analytics in fraud management.

A few decades ago, when banks first started accumulating data, databases quickly followed. Reporting became popular very quickly as well. In the absence of any information, when data is accumulated and some reports are run, it feels like lighting a candle in a dark room. The information seems extremely useful, and numbers-savvy people start looking at the reports and how some of the quantities (variables) in the report vary proportional to others. There is sometimes a direct correlation between fields; sometimes there is implied correlation. When domain experts start to see these correlations, relating these numbers to their own experience in risk management, they venture to write some rules to manage, say, fraud risk. These rules work effectively for a while but since they are rules, fraudsters become very good at figuring out what sort of fraud the rules are designed to stop. Fraudsters then figure out a way to fly below the radar. If the rule cutoff is $200 for a cash withdrawal, for example, the fraudster experiments with various amounts and determines that withdrawing $190 is a safe option. The domain experts see this and start designing rules that would catch this. In effect, it becomes a cat-and-mouse game between the fraud managers and fraudsters—a game that becomes an increasingly losing proposition for the fraud managers as fraudsters become increasingly crafty.

Now, here comes a data modeler who says that there is model that can effectively address this—a linear regression model. I am not going to give a lengthy description of what a linear regression model is, but it basically assumes that the relationships between the predictors used in the model and the fraud target are linear and tries to fit a linear model to detect fraud. Linear regression models provide significant lift over domain expert–driven rules as they systematically look at all data and can draw more effective conclusions than rules can.

What exactly are we trying to do when we go from a rule to a simple model to a more complex model? We are trying detect fraud better. One might ask: What exactly is meant by "detect fraud better"? Let's assume that 50 percent of a population has some fraudulent activity (this is too high a percentage in a real-life situation and is used for illustration purposes only) and 50 percent is clean. Suppose we have no analytic capability whatsoever and we resort to just flipping a coin to decide whether the transaction coming through is fraudulent or not. "Heads," we decide it is fraudulent; and "tails," we decide it is not. Let's look at the lift chart for this case. If we plot the percentage of transactions that are good or false alarms (false positives: good transactions that were misclassified as fraud) on the X-axis and the percentage of transactions that are fraud on the Y-axis, for the case when we flip the coin to decide, we end up with a diagonal line (the diagonal random dotted-and-dashed line in Figure 7.1). Basically, we are unable to identify a pool that is richer in fraud than the naturally occurring rate of fraud. So, we achieve no lift in fraud detection performance.

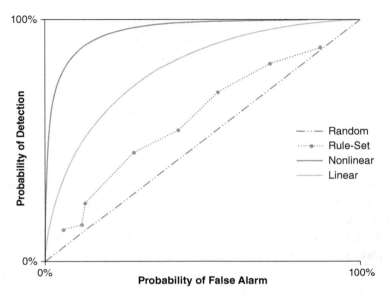

Figure 7.1 Probability of Detection versus Probability of False Alarm

When experts get together and devise a few rules, they can do slightly better than random chance in detecting fraud, but the rules may not cover the entire region of transactions. In other words, we may be able to give coverage for only a portion of the transactions (as represented in the shorter plotted curve in Figure 7.1). You can see that the dotted line with points along the line representing rules is above the diagonal line, which basically indicates that you can gain more percentage fraud (lift) in the pool of transactions toward the left end of the graph. In other words, it would be possible to identify a pool of transactions in which the percentage of fraud transactions is higher than the existing percentage of 50 percent fraud. It is not possible to get coverage for the overall space, but the points along the lines are realizable.

When we build a linear model using characteristics comparing past behavior with present behavior, it is typically possible to do better than the simple rules. There is an additional advantage of covering the entire set of transactions and classifying them as fraud or good. We can see that this line is above the rule line, which means that we can have a significantly higher percentage of fraud in a pool close to the left end

of the distribution. This is very desirable as the number of good transactions that we will have to take adverse action on decreases while
the number of fraud transactions increases in the pool. The lift above
random choice is higher in the case of a linear model compared to
simple rules.

With a nonlinear model, a significant increase in performance is
possible, thereby making the exercise of taking adverse action really
worth it. We can see that the blue line representing nonlinear model
is significantly above all the other lines. Points on these different
curves that correspond to specific values of the Probability of False
Alarm close to the origin clearly show that it is possible to do significantly better than the underlying fraud rate in some portions of the
transactions universe. In other words, it is possible to have a group
of transactions dominated by fraud transactions in which case it becomes easy to take adverse action on this pool of transactions. Also,
if a high portion of the fraud is detected as affecting a small portion
of the transactions, significant losses can be avoided. For every few
percentage points in fraud detected, it is possible for banks to save
millions of dollars (depending on the size of the portfolio). It is clear
from Figure 7.1 that the performance of the nonlinear model is the
best based on the lift observed.

In this chapter, we will use a very simple simulated example to
show the efficacy possible using sophisticated modeling algorithms.
The big drawback in using linear regression models for fraud is that,
in my experience building models for a number of risk phenomena,
I have not come across many cases where the underlying risk is truly
linear in its relationship to the predictors used in the model. The relationship is typically nonlinear. Also, linear regression tends to work
better in cases where both the target (fraud) and independent variables are continuous. Given that in fraud we are trying to predict a
dichotomous variable, a logistic regression model can be used to get
better results. While there are many problems where an 80 percent
solution is good enough, the fraud problem is not such a problem.
Increased complexity and sophistication are certainly worth it as the
effect on the bottom line can be substantial.

Going beyond logistic regression, nonlinear techniques such as
neural networks played a huge role in reducing false positives and

increasing fraud detection. Neural networks were originally devised to model the functioning of the brain. While they did not do very well in modeling brain functioning the nice statistical properties of neural networks made them an excellent fit for solving many risk problems. In recent times, there have been significant technological advancements above and beyond simple back-propagation neural networks that have yielded significantly better fraud detection results and hence reduction in fraud losses.

Generally, there are two schools of thought in building such models. One school believes that the technique doesn't matter that much; what matters is the data and how much variety one can get. There is some truth in this statement. There is certainly value to getting more data. There is significant gain to be had from getting better and more data. However, the other school believes that techniques do matter, and this position also deserves credit. There are several risk phenomena where improving the sophistication of the technique yields amazing results. Having spent almost two decades utilizing some of the most advanced techniques to extract value from the data, I thought it would be a good idea to show an example of how much value can be derived by the technique as opposed to the data. In this chapter, I will illustrate the benefit of using increasingly sophisticated techniques. For the sake of this illustration, I have simplified the fraud problem significantly. In real-life fraud modeling, this problem would be much more sophisticated and harder to solve.

A NOTE ABOUT THE DATA

The demo data used in the analyses for this example was generated synthetically to illustrate fraud models. Transactions were generated for about 100,000 fictitious accounts. The fraud rate was assumed to be 50 percent (in reality, fraud rates are 0.1 percent or less; 50 percent was chosen for illustrative purposes only), and the average transaction amount was assumed to be $100 with a variation of $20. Transaction dates, transaction times, transaction amounts, merchant category codes (MCCs), and point-of-sale (POS) codes were then randomly generated using some basic constraints to ensure reality of the synthetic data. Also, the riskiness of the MCCs; POS codes; and transaction amounts, dates, and times were constrained using our experience with fraud data over the last 15 to 20 years.

Correlations among these fields were also imposed; that is, some MCCs and POSs are more risky than others and hence are more likely to show up in compromised accounts. Similarly the frequency and transaction amount might behave differently for compromised accounts. On this data set, using three different variables that are decent indicators of fraud, individual linear regression, logistic regression, and neural network models were created. There was also a model that was run using all three variables as predictors. The results are given for each one of these runs. While real-world evaluation of fraud models involves many different quantities, we will look at the percentage of concordant predictions—basically how many frauds and non-frauds were classified using each technique. You will clearly see that neural networks yield better results than logistic regression, which does better than linear regression.

This is a single example of the same data being taken through multiple techniques to illustrate that nonlinear techniques can have significant advantage over linear techniques in detecting risk. A single example may not be conclusive in the reader's mind, but based on the experience of going through literally hundreds of modeling exercises, I can vouch for the validity of this example.

DATA

Let's start with the data. Here is the data set that was generated. The three variables we considered for the model (both individually as well as together) are the velocity of the transactions, avgMCCrsk—the average MCC risk associated with the transactions on the account, and avgPOSrsk—the average POS risk associated with the transactions on the account. While there are close to 100,000 observations in this data set, Table 7.1 shows the first 23 observations to give an idea of what the data looks like. The same experiment can be repeated with more variables.

In my experience, with most risk phenomena the technique does matter, even though the popularly held belief is that the technique doesn't matter. More sophisticated techniques certainly yield much

Table 7.1 The SAS System

obs	acctnum	frdtag	MCCtrx	POStrx	frstfrddate	blkdate	trxdt	auth_decn	trxtime	trxamt	velocity	avgMCCrsk	avgPOSrsk
1	6011300110025265	1	8999	81	06/02/2011	12/02/2011	12/02/2011	A	11:07:03	105.081	0.50000	6.3664	3.52716
2	6011300110045904	1	5734	1	12/01/2011	13/01/2011	13/01/2011	A	17:03:43	95.142	1.00000	12.3556	0.89403
3	6011300110095224	1	7372	1	12/02/2011	15/02/2011	15/02/2011	A	19:50:23	103.242	0.33333	9.2061	0.92622
4	6011300110185057	0	4816	80			04/06/2012	A	1:40:23.0	105.512	0.25000	6.8800	1.62000
5	6011300110245386	0	9999	90			17/11/2011	A	14:43:43	99.047	0.25000	1.0000	1.11000
6	6011300110275084	1	7399	1	19/01/2011	22/01/2011	22/01/2011	A	5:57:03.0	97.739	0.33333	6.2033	0.75867
7	6011300110285278	0	9999	0			28/09/2011	A	8:47:03.0	102.687	0.33333	1.0000	1.38000
8	6011300110315354	0	9999	2			18/09/2011	A	18:43:43	90.471	0.50000	1.0000	0.85000
9	6011300110355572	1	7311	1	03/01/2011	04/01/2011	04/01/2011	A	20:13:43	96.333	0.99900	7.2664	0.46848
10	6011300110455016	0	9999	79			04/06/2012	A	22:53:43	95.201	0.25000	1.0000	2.36000
11	6011300110485613	0	9999	5			05/02/2012	A	15:20:23	94.034	0.25000	1.0000	0.33000
12	6011300110905159	0	9999	5			14/07/2012	A	18:20:23	99.183	0.25000	1.0000	0.33000
13	6011300110945962	1	7399	1	21/01/2011	22/01/2011	22/01/2011	A	12:30:23	102.313	1.00000	6.7562	0.95115
14	6011300111035036	0	9999	2			05/02/2012	A	2:50:23.0	91.443	0.25000	1.0000	0.85000
15	6011300111125495	0	9999	7			27/12/2011	A	11:33:43	102.508	0.25000	1.0000	0.11000
16	6011300111196554	1	7311	1	06/02/2011	12/02/2011	12/02/2011	A	21:13:43	104.674	0.33333	10.9850	0.91778
17	6011300111475348	0	9999	80			05/02/2012	A	2:50:23.0	105.151	0.25000	1.0000	1.62000
18	6011300111515384	0	9999	95			05/02/2012	A	13:57:03	104.957	0.25000	1.0000	0.10000
19	6011300111695090	0	9999	7			16/03/2012	A	13:33:43	98.372	0.25000	1.0000	0.11000
20	6011300111695296	1	7399	81	07/01/2011	25/01/2011	25/01/2011	A	7:20:23.0	95.757	0.33333	6.3703	2.96273
21	6011300111945858	1	7311	1	16/04/2011	19/04/2011	19/04/2011	A	17:40:23	96.428	0.33333	11.0600	0.95969
22	6011300111945907	0	9999	1			05/02/2012	A	2:50:23.0	99.008	0.25000	1.0000	0.96000
23	6011300111985239	1	8999	81	03/01/2011	07/01/2011	07/01/2011	A	20:13:43	96.137	0.49950	4.1851	1.73728

better results compared to simpler techniques. This is most likely due to the nonlinear nature of these risk phenomena. Only if the fundamental relationship between the target and the independent variables is linear will more sophisticated nonlinear approaches be unlikely to yield superior results. This subtle difference is sometimes lost on users of models.

I have come across users who swear by the specific technique of modeling they use; I have also come across users who are total believers that data is everything and the technique doesn't matter. The truth is somewhere in between. Without data nothing much useful can be achieved. However, depending on the problem, using the right technique can be extremely important. This argument is similar to choosing whether climbing gear or goggles are more important while climbing a treacherous, snowy peak. Climbing gear is extremely important but even with the best climbing gear, if the snow is blinding the climber, without the goggles, the climb can result in disastrous results. I am always amused by the arguments about technique versus data that I witness in customer meetings. Both are important to varying degrees depending on the nature of the problem.

Statistics

We generated statistics on this data set to gain a better understanding of how the variables are distributed. There are various MCCs in the system, and the results of running the FREQ procedure in SAS are shown in Tables 7.2 and 7.3. The output of running the means procedure on SAS on the three predictor variables is shown in Table 7.4.

REGRESSION 1

Tables 7.5 through 7.8 illustrate a regression model that was built using velocity as the independent variable. The R-square d which represents the fraction of the variation in the data explained by the model achieved (0.36) is decent, but we will attempt to improve it by using logistic regression and neural network models. The progressive improvement becomes obvious by looking at the percent age of cases that are concordant.

Table 7.2 The FREQ Procedure

Table of frdtag by MCCtrx

Frequency Percent Row Pct Col Pct											
FrdTag					MCCtrx						Total
	4816	5310	5734	5965	5967	7311	7372	7399	8999	9999	
0	51820	55380	55630	58250	57840	52250	56630	56670	51840	4966600	5462910
	0.85	0.91	0.92	0.96	0.95	0.86	0.93	0.93	0.85	81.80	89.97
	0.95	1.01	1.02	1.07	1.06	0.96	1.04	1.04	0.95	90.91	
	45.20	47.00	47.87	49.64	48.31	46.10	48.04	48.57	46.74	98.79	
1	62836	62439	60578	59088	61891	61088	61263	59998	59073	60755	609009
	1.03	1.03	1.00	0.97	1.02	1.01	1.01	0.99	0.97	1.00	10.03
	10.32	10.25	9.95	9.70	10.16	10.03	10.06	9.85	9.70	9.98	
	54.80	53.00	52.13	50.36	51.69	53.90	51.96	51.43	53.26	1.21	
Total	114656	117819	116208	117338	119731	113338	117893	116668	110913	5027355	6071919
	1.89	1.94	1.91	1.93	1.97	1.87	1.94	1.92	1.83	82.80	100.00

Frequency Missing = 8

129

Table 7.3 Table of frdtag by POStrx

Table of frdtag by POStrx

Frequency Percent Row Pct Col Pct	POStrx										Total
frdtag	0	1	2	5	7	79	80	81	90	95	
0	552490	549660	549200	529550	551340	547950	553590	555340	538750	535040	5462910
	9.10	9.05	9.04	8.72	9.08	9.02	9.12	9.15	8.87	8.81	89.97
	10.11	10.06	10.05	9.69	10.09	10.03	10.13	10.17	9.86	9.79	
	96.73	69.40	97.80	97.73	97.86	96.66	96.61	69.60	96.81	97.70	
1	18666	242328	12349	12326	12046	18950	19452	242516	17776	12600	609009
	0.31	3.99	0.20	0.20	0.20	0.31	0.32	3.99	0.29	0.21	10.03
	3.06	39.79	2.03	2.02	1.98	3.11	3.19	39.82	2.92	2.07	
	3.27	30.60	2.20	2.27	2.14	3.34	3.39	30.40	3.19	2.30	
Total	571156	791988	561549	541876	563386	566900	573042	797856	556526	547640	6071919
	9.41	13.04	9.25	8.92	9.28	9.34	9.44	13.14	9.17	9.02	100.00

Frequency Missing = 8

130

Table 7.4 The MEANS Procedure

frdtag	N Obs	Variable	N	Mean	Std Dev	Minimum	Maximum
0	50131	Velocity	50131	0.3043110	0.1693025	0.2500000	1.0000000
		avgMCCrsk	50131	1.9584120	4.4226245	1.0000000	39.9900000
		avgPOSrsk	50131	1.2452142	1.0245354	0.0999998	3.5600000
1	49866	velocity	49866	0.6565705	0.2859493	0.3300000	1.0000000
		avgMCCrsk	49866	9.2880741	9.5481060	0.5100000	39.9900000
		avgPOSrsk	49866	1.6480048	1.1410180	0.0360000	3.5600000

Table 7.5 The REG Procedure

Model: MODEL1	
Dependent Variable: frdtag	
Number of Observations Read	99997
Number of Observations Used	99997

Table 7.6 Analysis of Variance

Analysis of Variance					
Source	DF	Sum of Squares	Mean Square	F Value	Pr > F
Model	1	9000.24797	9000.24797	56252.9	<.0001
Error	99995	15999	0.16000		
Corrected Total	99996	24999			

Table 7.7 Root MSE, Dependent Mean, CoeffVar

Root MSE	0.40000	R-Square	0.3600
Dependent Mean	0.49867	Adj R-Sq	0.3600
CoeffVar	80.21163		

Table 7.8 Parameter Estimates

Parameter Estimates					
Variable	DF	Parameter Estimate	Standard Error	t Value	Pr > |t|
Intercept	1	0.00812	0.00242	3.35	0.0008
Velocity	1	1.02204	0.00431	237.18	<.0001

LOGISTIC REGRESSION 1

Tables 7.9 through 7.18 use velocity as the independent variable but the model run is logistic regression. The results are certainly better than what we observe in linear regression.

Table 7.9 The LOGISTIC Procedure

Model Information	
Data Set	DEMO.MODELVARS
Response Variable	Frdtag
Number of Response Levels	2
Model	binary logit
Optimization Technique	Fisher's scoring

Table 7.10 Observations Read versus Observations Used

Number of Observations Read	99997
Number of Observations Used	99997

Table 7.11 Response Profile

Response Profile		
Ordered Value	frdtag	Total Frequency
1	0	50131
2	1	49866

Table 7.12 Probability modeled is frdtag = 0.

Model Convergence Status
Convergence criterion (GCONV = 1E-8) satisfied.

Table 7.13 Model Fit Statistics

Model Fit Statistics		
Criterion	Intercept Only	Intercept and Covariates
AIC	138626.57	92934.155

Table 7.14 R-Square and Max-rescaled R-Square

R-Square	0.3668	Max-rescaled R-Square	0.4891

Table 7.15 Testing Global Null Hypothesis

Testing Global Null Hypothesis: BETA = 0			
Test	Chi-Square	DF	Pr > ChiSq
Likelihood Ratio	45694.4202	1	<.0001
Score	36001.2447	1	<.0001
Wald	16408.3865	1	<.0001

Table 7.16 Analysis of Maximum Likelihood Estimates

Analysis of Maximum Likelihood Estimates					
Parameter	DF	Estimate	Standard Error	Wald Chi-Square	Pr > ChiSq
Intercept	1	3.1739	0.0226	19798.0951	<.0001
Velocity	1	−7.6473	0.0597	16408.3865	<.0001

Table 7.17 Odds Ratio Estimates

Odds Ratio Estimates			
Effect	Point Estimate	95% Wald Confidence Limits	
Velocity	<0.001	<0.001	<0.001

Table 7.18 Association of Predicted Probabilities and Observed Responses

Association of Predicted Probabilities and Observed Responses			
Percent Concordant	90.7	Somers' D	0.862
Percent Discordant	4.5	Gamma	0.905
Percent Tied	4.8	Tau-a	0.431
Pairs	2499832446	c	0.931

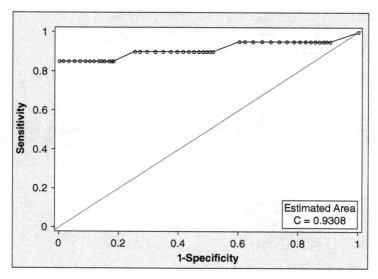

Figure 7.2 ROC Curve for logistic 1

Neural Network 1

This neural network model is shown in Tables 7.19 through 7.21 and uses velocity as the independent variable. There is a clear drop in the misclassification rate when we go from a logistic regression model to a neural network, and this drop in misclassification rate is very desirable.

Regression 2

Regression model 2 (Tables 7.22 through 7.25) is run with avgMCCrsk as the independent variable. This independent variable is weaker in predicting fraud than velocity. However, in this case as well, it is clear that there is improvement in the models as we go from linear regression to logistic regression to neural network. It is very interesting to observe that even with a weak predictor (independent variable), technique seems to matter.

Table 7.19 The NEURAL Procedure

	Optimization Start		
Parameter Estimates			
N	Parameter	Estimate	Gradient Objective Function
1	velocity_H11	−0.295500	0
2	velocity_H12	−0.629577	0
3	velocity_H13	0.121411	0
4	BIAS_H11	−1.333728	0
5	BIAS_H12	−1.565237	0
6	BIAS_H13	−0.642139	0
7	H11_frdtag0	0	−0.020062
8	H12_frdtag0	0	−0.030288
9	H13_frdtag0	0	0.025587
10	BIAS_frdtag0	0.005300	−4.58618E-15

Table 7.20 Value of Objective Function = 0.6931436691

Train: Akaike's Information Criterion	Train: Average Squared Error	Train: Maximum Absolute Error	Train: Root Final Prediction Error	Train: Misclassification Rate	Train: Number of Wrong Classifications
.	0.06551	0.88079	0.25598	0.075742	7574
44606.92	0.06551	0.88079	0.25598	0.075742	7574

Table 7.21 The FREQ Procedure

Frequency Percent	Table of F_frdtag by I_frdtag			
	F_frdtag(From: frdtag)	I_frdtag(Into: frdtag)		Total
		0	1	
Row Pct	0	42557 42.56 84.89 100.00	7574 7.57 15.11 13.19	50131 50.13
Col Pct	1	0 0.00 0.00 0.00	49866 49.87 100.00 86.81	49866 49.87
	Total	42557 42.56	57440 57.44	99997 100.00

Table 7.22 The REG Procedure

Model: MODEL1	
Dependent Variable: frdtag	
Number of Observations Read	99997
Number of Observations Used	99997

Table 7.23 Analysis of Variance

Analysis of Variance					
Source	DF	Sum of Squares	Mean Square	F Value	Pr > F
Model	1	4887.48595	4887.48595	24300.6	<.0001
Error	99995	20112	0.20113		
Corrected Total	99996	24999			

Table 7.24 Root MSE, Dependent Mean, CoeffVar

Root MSE	0.44847	R-Square	0.1955
Dependent Mean	0.49867	Adj R-Sq	0.1955
CoeffVar	89.93246		

Table 7.25 Parameter Estimates

Parameter Estimates					
Variable	DF	Parameter Estimate	Standard Error	t Value	Pr > |t|
Intercept	1	0.34894	0.00171	203.72	<.0001
avgMCCrsk	1	0.02667	0.00017111	155.89	<.0001

Logistic Regression 2

This is a logistic regression model run with avgMCCrsk as the independent variable. It is clear that the R-square is better than what we observed for the linear regression model on the same variable. The results of this logistic regression are given in Tables 7.26 -7.35.

Table 7.26 The LOGISTIC Procedure

Model Information	
Data Set	DEMO.MODELVARS
Response Variable	frdtag
Number of Response Levels	2
Model	binary logit
Optimization Technique	Fisher's scoring

Table 7.27 Observations Read versus Observations Used

Number of Observations Read	99997
Number of Observations Used	99997

Table 7.28 Response Profile

Response Profile		
Ordered Value	Frdtag	Total Frequency
1	0	50131
2	1	49866

Table 7.29 Probability Modeled is frdtag = 0.

Model Convergence Status
Convergence criterion (GCONV = 1E-8) satisfied

Table 7.30 Model Fit Statistics

Model Fit Statistics		
Criterion	Intercept Only	Intercept and Covariates
AIC	138626.57	96756.624
SC	138636.09	96775.650
-2 Log L	138624.57	96752.624

Table 7.31 R-Square and Max-rescaled R-Square

R-Square	0.3421	Max-rescaled R-Square	0.4562

Table 7.32 Testing Global Null Hypothesis

Testing Global Null Hypothesis: BETA = 0			
Test	Chi-Square	DF	Pr > ChiSq
Likelihood Ratio	41871.9506	1	<.0001
Score	19550.0811	1	<.0001
Wald	21579.8183	1	<.0001

Table 7.33 Analysis of Maximum Likelihood Estimates

Analysis of Maximum Likelihood Estimates					
Parameter	DF	Estimate	Standard Error	Wald Chi-Square	Pr > ChiSq
Intercept	1	1.6564	0.0121	18665.4780	<.0001
avgMCCrsk	1	−0.4327	0.00295	21579.8183	<.0001

Table 7.34 Odds Ratio Estimates

Odds Ratio Estimates			
Effect	Point Estimate	95% Wald Confidence Limits	
avgMCCrsk	0.649	0.645	0.653

Table 7.35 Association of Predicted Probabilities and Observed Responses

Association of Predicted Probabilities and Observed Responses			
Percent Concordant	85.0	Somers' D	0.740
Percent Discordant	11.0	Gamma	0.771
Percent Tied	4.0	Tau-a	0.370
Pairs	2499832446	c	0.870

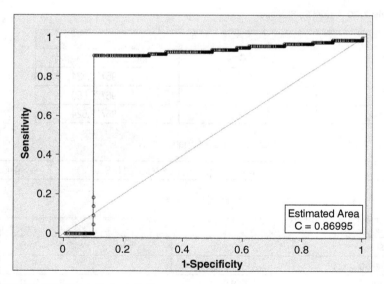

Figure 7.3 ROC Curve for Logistic 2

Neural Network 2

Tables 7.36 through 7.38 show the results of a neural network model run using avgMCCrsk as the independent variable. The improvement is clearly evident.

Table 7.36 The NEURAL Procedure

Optimization Start			
Parameter Estimates			
N	Parameter	Estimate	Gradient Objective Function
1	avgMCCrsk_H11	−0.295500	0
2	avgMCCrsk_H12	−0.629577	0
3	avgMCCrsk_H13	0.121411	0
4	BIAS_H11	−1.333728	0
5	BIAS_H12	−1.565237	0
6	BIAS_H13	−0.642139	0
7	H11_frdtag0	0	−0.013438
8	H12_frdtag0	0	−0.019327
9	H13_frdtag0	0	0.019547
10	BIAS_frdtag0	0.005300	−4.58618E-15

Table 7.37 Train: Criterion, Errors, Rate, Classifications

Train: Akaike's Information Criterion	Train: Average Squared Error	Train: Maximum Absolute Error	Train: Root Final Prediction Error	Train: Misclassification Rate	Train: Number of Wrong Classifications
.	0.08657	0.91893	0.29426	0.095613	9561
63203.51	0.08657	0.91893	0.29426	0.095613	9561

Table 7.38 The FREQ Procedure

Frequency Percent	Table of F_frdtag by I_frdtag			
	F_frdtag(From: frdtag)	I_frdtag(Into: frdtag)		Total
		0	1	
Row Pct	0	45573 45.57 90.91 90.11	4558 4.56 9.09 9.22	50131 50.13
Col Pct	1	5003 5.00 10.03 9.89	44863 44.86 89.97 90.78	49866 49.87
	Total	50576 50.58	49421 49.42	99997 100.00

Regression 3

Regression model 3 was run using avgPOSrsk as the dependent variable, and is shown in Tables 7.39 through 7.42. The relationship to the fraud tag is not very strong. However, again in this case we can see progressive improvement in model performance as we move from linear regression to logistic regression to neural network model.

Table 7.39 The REG Procedure

Model: MODEL1	
Dependent Variable: frdtag	
Number of Observations Read	99997
Number of Observations Used	99997

Table 7.40 Analysis of Variance

Analysis of Variance					
Source	DF	Sum of Squares	Mean Square	F Value	Pr > F
Model	1	833.84648	833.84648	3450.43	<.0001
Error	99995	24165	0.24166		
Corrected Total	99996	24999			

Table 7.41 Root MSE, Dependent Mean, CoeffVar

Root MSE	0.49159	R-Square	0.0334
Dependent Mean	0.49867	Adj R-Sq	0.0333
CoeffVar	98.57998		

Table 7.42 Parameter Estimates

Parameter Estimates					
Variable	DF	Parameter Estimate	Standard Error	t Value	Pr > |t|
Intercept	1	0.37893	0.00256	147.80	<.0001
avgPOSrsk	1	0.08281	0.00141	58.74	<.0001

Logistic Regression 3

Logistic regression model 3 uses the same independent variable (avgPOSrsk) and is shown in Tables 7.43 to 7.52.

Table 7.43 The LOGISTIC Procedure

Model Information	
Data Set	DEMO.MODELVARS
Response Variable	frdtag
Number of Response Levels	2
Model	binary logit
Optimization Technique	Fisher's scoring

Table 7.44 Observations Read versus Observations Used

Number of Observations Read	99997
Number of Observations Used	99997

Table 7.45 Response Profile

Response Profile		
Ordered Value	frdtag	Total Frequency
1	0	50131
2	1	49866

Table 7.46 Probability Modeled is frdtag = 0.

Model Convergence Status
Convergence criterion (GCONV = 1E-8) satisfied.

Table 7.47 Model Fit Statistics

Model Fit Statistics		
Criterion	Intercept Only	Intercept and Covariates
AIC	138626.57	135250.36
SC	138636.09	135269.38
−2 Log L	138624.57	135246.36

Table 7.48 R-Square versus Max-rescaled R-Square

R-Square	0.0332	Max-rescaled R-Square	0.0443

Table 7.49 Testing Global Null Hypothesis

Testing Global Null Hypothesis: BETA = 0			
Test	Chi-Square	DF	Pr > ChiSq
Likelihood Ratio	3378.2165	1	<.0001
Score	3335.4094	1	<.0001
Wald	3247.7672	1	<.0001

Table 7.50 Analysis of Maximum Likelihood Estimates

Analysis of Maximum Likelihood Estimates					
Parameter	DF	Estimate	Standard Error	Wald Chi-Square	Pr > ChiSq
Intercept	1	0.4939	0.0106	2156.3435	<.0001
avgPOSrsk	1	−0.3399	0.00596	3247.7672	<.0001

Table 7.51 Odds Ratio Estimates

Odds Ratio Estimates			
Effect	Point Estimate	95% Wald Confidence Limits	
avgPOSrsk	0.712	0.704	0.720

Table 7.52 Association of Predicted Probabilities and Observed Responses

Association of Predicted Probabilities and Observed Responses			
Percent Concordant	56.2	Somers' D	0.142
Percent Discordant	42.1	Gamma	0.144
Percent Tied	1.7	Tau-a	0.071
Pairs	2499832446	C	0.571

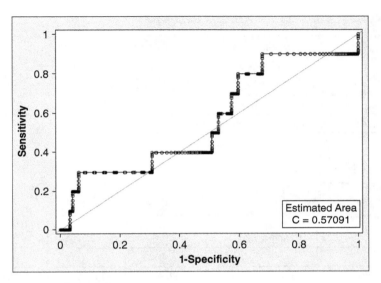

Figure 7.4 ROC for Logistic 3

Neural Network 3

Neural network 3 uses the same independent variable (avgPOSrsk), and is shown in Tables 7.53 through 7.55. There is significant improvement in the misclassification rate compared to the logistic regression model.

Table 7.53 The NEURAL Procedure

Optimization Start			
Parameter Estimates			
N	Parameter	Estimate	Gradient Objective Function
1	avgPOSrsk_H11	−0.295500	0
2	avgPOSrsk_H12	−0.629577	0
3	avgPOSrsk_H13	0.121411	0
4	BIAS_H11	−1.333728	0
5	BIAS_H12	−1.565237	0
6	BIAS_H13	−0.642139	0
7	H11_frdtag0	0	−0.006142
8	H12_frdtag0	0	−0.010035
9	H13_frdtag0	0	0.007817
10	BIAS_frdtag0	0.005300	−4.58618E-15

Table 7.54 Value of Objective Function = 0.6931436691

Train: Akaike's Information Criterion	Train: Average Squared Error	Train: Maximum Absolute Error	Train: Root Final Prediction Error	Train: Misclassification Rate	Train: Number of Wrong Classifications
.	0.19668	0.91596	0.44353	0.33134	33133
114124.63	0.19668	0.91596	0.44353	0.33134	33133

Table 7.55 The FREQ Procedure

Frequency Percent	Table of F_frdtag by I_frdtag			
	F_frdtag (From: frdtag)	I_frdtag(Into: frdtag)		Total
		0	1	
Row Pct	0	34979 34.98 69.78 66.05	15152 15.15 30.22 32.21	50131 50.13
Col Pct	1	17981 17.98 36.06 33.95	31885 31.89 63.94 67.79	49866 49.87
	Total	52960 52.96	47037 47.04	99997 100.00

Regression 4

Regression model 4 (Tables 7.56 through 7.59) uses all three independent variables to predict fraud. The results are of course much better. However, in this case as well, we see that the results are progressively better as we go through different techniques.

Table 7.56 The REG Procedure

Model: MODEL1	
Dependent Variable: frdtag	
Number of Observations Read	99997
Number of Observations Used	99997

Table 7.57 Analysis of Variance

Analysis of Variance					
Source	DF	Sum of Squares	Mean Square	F Value	Pr > F
Model	3	11320	3773.27059	27581.9	<.0001
Error	99993	13679	0.13680		
Corrected Total	99996	24999			

Table 7.58 Root MSE, Dependent Mean, CoeffVar

Root MSE	0.36987	R-Square	0.4528
Dependent Mean	0.49867	Adj R-Sq	0.4528
CoeffVar	74.17012		

Table 7.59 Parameter Estimates

Parameter Estimates					
Variable	DF	Parameter Estimate	Standard Error	t Value	Pr > |t|
Intercept	1	−0.07721	0.00261	−29.61	<.0001
Velocity	1	0.86913	0.00415	209.22	<.0001
avgMCCrsk	1	0.01777	0.00014708	120.79	<.0001
avgPOSrsk	1	0.04079	0.00107	38.06	<.0001

Logistic Regression 4

Logistic regression model 4 (Tables 7.60–7.68) uses all three independent variables to predict fraud tag.

Table 7.60 The LOGISTIC Procedure

Model Information	
Data Set	DEMO.MODELVARS
Response Variable	frdtag
Number of Response Levels	2
Model	binary logit
Optimization Technique	Fisher's scoring

Table 7.61 Observations Read versus Observations Used

Number of Observations Read	99997
Number of Observations Used	99997

Table 7.62 Response Profile

Response Profile		
Ordered Value	frdtag	Total Frequency
1	0	50131
2	1	49866

Table 7.63 Probability modeled is frdtag = 0.

Model Convergence Status		
Convergence criterion (GCONV = 1E-8) satisfied		
Model Fit Statistics		
Criterion	Intercept Only	Intercept and Covariates
AIC	138626.57	72379.668
SC	138636.09	72417.719
−2 Log L	138624.57	72371.668

Table 7.64 R-Square versus Max-rescaled R-Square

R-Square	0.4845	Max-rescaled R-Square	0.6460

Table 7.65 Testing Global Null Hypothesis

Testing Global Null Hypothesis: BETA = 0			
Test	Chi-Square	DF	Pr > ChiSq
Likelihood Ratio	66252.9074	3	<.0001
Score	45279.5651	3	<.0001
Wald	27436.3946	3	<.0001

Table 7.66 Analysis of Maximum Likelihood Estimates

Analysis of Maximum Likelihood Estimates					
Parameter	DF	Estimate	Standard Error	Wald Chi-Square	Pr > ChiSq
Intercept	1	4.1144	0.0267	23742.4387	<.0001
velocity	1	−5.6355	0.0500	12727.9519	<.0001
avgMCCrsk	1	−0.3149	0.00304	10751.6046	<.0001
avgPOSrsk	1	−0.2588	0.00866	893.6669	<.0001

Table 7.67 Odds Ratio Estimates

Odds Ratio Estimates			
Effect	Point Estimate	95% Wald Confidence Limits	
velocity	0.004	0.003	0.004
avgMCCrsk	0.730	0.726	0.734
avgPOSrsk	0.772	0.759	0.785

Table 7.68 Association of Predicted Probabilities and Observed Responses

Association of Predicted Probabilities and Observed Responses			
Percent Concordant	94.3	Somers' D	0.889
Percent Discordant	5.5	Gamma	0.890
Percent Tied	0.2	Tau-a	0.444
Pairs	2499832446	C	0.944

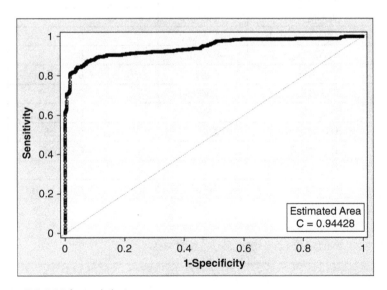

Figure 7.5 ROC for Logistic 4

Neural Network 4

Neural network 4 (Tables 7.69–7.71) uses all three independent variables to predict risk. As you can see, there is significant reduction in misclassification rate when we use a neural network compared to a logistic regression model even though the logistic regression model performs very well in absolute terms.

Table 7.69 The NEURAL Procedure

Optimization Start			
Parameter Estimates			
N	Parameter	Estimate	Gradient Objective Function
1	velocity_H11	−0.170607	0
2	avgMCCrsk_H11	−0.363486	0
3	avgPOSrsk_H11	0.070097	0
4	velocity_H12	−0.770028	0
5	avgMCCrsk_H12	−0.903690	0
6	avgPOSrsk_H12	−0.370739	0
7	velocity_H13	0.860670	0
8	avgMCCrsk_H13	−1.256862	0
9	avgPOSrsk_H13	−0.772025	0
10	BIAS_H11	−0.199277	0
11	BIAS_H12	−1.348886	0
12	BIAS_H13	−0.613004	0
13	H11_frdtag0	0	−0.103956
14	H12_frdtag0	0	−0.155604
15	H13_frdtag0	0	−0.001968
16	BIAS_frdtag0	0.005300	−4.58618E-15

Table 7.70 Value of Objective Function = 0.6931436691

Train: Akaike's Information Criterion	Train: Average Squared Error	Train: Maximum Absolute Error	Train: Root Final Prediction Error	Train: Misclassification Rate	Train: Number of Wrong Classifications
.	0.02020	0.98527	0.14216	0.024681	2468
15835.88	0.02020	0.98527	0.14216	0.024681	2468

Table 7.71 The FREQ Procedure

Frequency Percent	Table of F_frdtag by I_frdtag		
	F_frdtag(From: frdtag)	I_frdtag(Into: frdtag)	Total
		0	1	
Row Pct	0	49401 49.40 98.54 96.60	730 0.73 1.46 1.49	50131 50.13
Col Pct	1	1738 1.74 3.49 3.40	48128 48.13 96.51 98.51	49866 49.87
	Total	51139 51.14	48858 48.86	99997 100.00

"MODELS SHOULD BE AS SIMPLE AS POSSIBLE, BUT NOT SIMPLER"

I read somewhere that analytics literally means the science of analysis but in practical terms, it is the systematic process of developing decision recommendations based on insights gathered using statistical analysis of past data and combining it with practical considerations and intuition. Based on this chapter's simple example (with all applicable caveats), the insights gathered certainly seem to improve significantly as we apply more and more sophisticated techniques to the data. Paraphrasing a quote attributed to Einstein: "Models should be as simple as possible, but not simpler."

I interpret this statement as follows: While there is considerable merit in keeping the models simple, they shouldn't be made simpler than they need to be. If we look at the latest iteration (number 4) that we tried using all three independent variables, using the exact same variables and simply changing the method to a neural network instead of a logistic regression, we can reduce the misclassification rate from 5.7 to 2.5 percent. This is a significant reduction in misclassification rate and in real-world fraud detection, and this lift can result in huge monetary benefit. Why is a neural network more effective in detecting fraud? It is simply because neural networks have a nonzero probability of including variable interactions in the models without the modeler having to find the interactions that are useful and code them into the model. In a nonlinear phenomenon, it is hard for a logistic regression model to do better than a neural network model.

In the real world, the underlying fraud rates are much lower than what we have in this synthetic data set. The fraud rates observed are 1/10 of 1 percent or less. The fraud rate in this data set is 50 percent. When we observe the ROC curves for the logistic regression models, it will become clear to us that even though the R-square values look decent, the model is not that effective in the region where it matters, namely the left end of the distribution on the graph. In recent times, sophistication way beyond what is used in simple back-propagation neural networks has been introduced successfully, yielding tremendous improvement in fraud detection.

As technologies improve, the methods fraudsters use to defraud banks are also bound to improve. In this race to combat fraud, it is essential that banks keep a few steps ahead of the fraudsters. This requires the ability to obtain and incorporate new sources of data quickly into fraud detection systems. Introducing new data cannot mean a total overhaul and reinstall of the fraud detection system. Banks simply can't afford to do this. The good news in this area is that current fraud detection systems have the ability to take in data that was not conceived to be part of the system when it was implemented. It is important for banks to consider the data incorporation angle when choosing a system.

In addition to this, the ability to score and react to all transactions in real time is a requirement as well. Scoring all transactions in real time is helpful not only in detecting fraud more effectively but also in reducing annoyance to good customers. We also need to constantly explore new techniques of extracting information from the data as well as new methods of modeling the fraud phenomena.

I believe strongly that in terms of using advanced analytical techniques, as exciting as the improvements in performance of fraud models have been in the recent past, we are simply scratching the surface. As data proliferates and the time to react gets squeezed more and more, sophistication is going to make a lot of these problems solvable, and banks as well as customers are going to get more and more demanding with respect to analytical techniques.

SUMMARY

As a statistician by training, I have watched the emerging fields of data mining and machine learning and the new generation of data scientists. The ability exhibited by some of these folks to understand and organize data is very commendable. However, I would like to remind the reader that the science of making sense of data is strongly rooted in the principles of statistics. Different disciplines call it by different names—data mining, pattern recognition, or the like. If we evaluate what is at the heart of looking at data and making sense of it, statistical principles are the main drivers. When statistical principles are not the main drivers of these techniques, it leads to a worrisome path. Dr. Vijay Desai, a longtime associate of mine, once said, "Isn't machine learning the phenomenon of computer scientists rediscovering statistics all over again?" I do not worry about the name by which we call it as long as we recognize the statistical principles behind data analysis and use them with rigor. Techniques developed with this in mind are going to make the data world very exciting. We are just getting started on this path.

CHAPTER **8**

The Proof of the Pudding May Not Be in the Eating

I am a fan not only of Leonardo da Vinci's paintings but also the quotes attributed to him. Two quotes come to mind. The first one is: "I have been impressed with the urgency of doing. Knowing is not enough; we must apply. Being willing is not enough; we must do."[1] The second one is: "Simplicity is the ultimate sophistication."[2] When I dug into these quotes a bit more, I discovered that they are actually from Russell C. Taylor and William Gaddis, respectively.

The first quote, though, is extremely relevant to fraud management. We need to *know* what is important, and also we need to *apply our knowledge* in a timely fashion. The passage of time between banks learning something and banks implementing this learning in production has to get shorter and shorter. *Doing* in a timely fashion determines whether fraud can be tackled successfully or not.

Luckily there are technologically advanced fraud detection solutions on the market today that afford the ability to add new data, learn patterns on the fly, incorporate fraud outcome into the production model, keep track of multiple entities simultaneously, and the like. Such solutions will significantly shorten the time between the acquisition of knowledge and using the knowledge in production. The ability to create and deploy rules in production rapidly is also a key requirement. If an ongoing fraud pattern emerges but if it takes several days to create the operational rule, test the rule, and move the rule into production, the rule may be obsolete by the time it gets implemented. Speed in the upkeep of the models and the operational rules is not a luxury anymore. It is a key requirement of any good fraud detection system.

You might be wondering what the title of this chapter is referring to—"The Proof of the Pudding May Not Be in the Eating." This is related to the Gaddis quote, "Simplicity is the ultimate sophistication." This applies to most situations in life. However, when it comes to introducing new fraud management systems, simplicity in understanding production results may lead to a lot of confusion instead of providing clarity. A significant level of sophistication is necessary to understand production fraud model performance—this is due partially to fraud being a censored problem and partially to the complexities in the measurement of fraud losses, even the ones incurred and recorded well. This chapter will look into some of the unique challenges associated with understanding fraud model performance.

UNDERSTANDING PRODUCTION FRAUD MODEL PERFORMANCE

One of the most counterintuitive situations in risk management is when a new system is introduced and the fraud losses (or losses from other risk) go higher. The "obvious" conclusion is to assume that the new fraud management system is not doing a very good job. Similarly, if a new system gets introduced and let us say the fraud losses go down, we might wrongly conclude that the system is extremely good at reducing fraud losses. Both these situations can lead to the wrong conclusions by fraud managers. This is just one of many misconceptions in fraud management. The censored nature of fraud accentuates this issue. In this chapter, I will discuss a few such issues and how they can be effectively avoided.

THE SCIENCE OF QUALITY CONTROL

Before we examine issues specific to fraud management, it might be relevant to look at the science of quality control. Quality control measures were at least loosely applied in early historic times. As early as 3000 B.C., Hammurabi, the ruler of Babylonia, is believed to have said, "If a builder builds a house for a man and does not make its construction firm, and the house which he has built collapses and causes the death of the owner of the home, that builder shall be put to death."[3] Ancient Greek architecture also had very strict quality control standards. However, quality control—the way we know it today with large-scale applications—started around the time of the Industrial Revolution. Later, in the 1920s, Bell Labs physicist Walter Shewart introduced statistical quality control measures, and these methods were quickly adopted by various manufacturing units. Japanese quality control methods from around that time are world famous and gave their products an amazing reputation of reliability. However, when these systematic measures were introduced, initially a lot of defects were identified. This made some of the skeptics wonder if these quality control measures were somehow introducing more problems into the process. It took a while for people to understand that defects that would have gone unnoticed earlier were now being identified and effectively stopped.

The reader might not immediately see the connection between quality control and fraud management, but there are a lot of similarities. Let's consider the following case: The fraud management system you have in place identifies about 40 percent of all the fraud at a 20:1 false positive ratio. If you introduce a fraud management system that is far superior to the current system—say with 60 percent fraud detection at a 20:1 false positive ratio—the most likely immediate outcome is a tremendous increase in fraud losses in the first few months. This is because the fraud that used to be identified only when the customer called and reported it (which might have been up to four months after the actual fraud episode) is now getting identified and stopped by the system within a short period of the fraud episode happening. It is also getting recorded as fraud loss, creating some angst among fraud managers.

FALSE POSITIVE RATIOS

The other side of this is also interesting. Let's say you have a system capable of identifying 40 percent of all the fraud losses at a 20:1 false positive ratio. You introduce a new system that has a promise of detecting 45 percent of all the fraud losses at a 20:1 false positive ratio. Let us say in reality, the performance of the new system is only 30 percent at a 20:1 false positive ratio. Since the new system catches significantly less fraud than the old system, the fraud losses will drop in the beginning. If this makes the fraud manager conclude that the new system is working very well, there will be valuable time lost in correcting the new system. Any risk management system with much higher efficacy will identify more risk in the beginning. This should not be mistaken as a weakness with the current system. While this confusion is likely to exist for only a short period of time, it is certainly something to watch out for.

Most fraud episodes that go unidentified can take up to four months (sometimes longer) to get reported. In the meantime, it would be a very good idea to get estimates of the likely fraud losses based on historic numbers and use some extrapolations where applicable to estimate the losses that are likely to come in.

MEASUREMENT OF FRAUD DETECTION AGAINST ACCOUNT FALSE POSITIVE RATIO

Another interesting quandary in fraud management is the measurement of fraud detection against account false positive ratio (AFPR). There are typically two different types of detection that are used to measure fraud models: fraud account detection and fraud monetary loss detection. AFPR can help in understanding operational impact by predicting what proportion of the outbound calls (based on the system flagging transactions as suspicious) will result in fraud detection. The problem with this quantity is that it is a ratio of two quantities and hides the actual numbers behind the ratio. When we consider fraud account detection measured against AFPR to determine the efficacy of a model, we can end up with erroneous conclusions, especially when we are comparing two models.

Let's take this simple example. We are looking at a portfolio of 1,000,000 accounts with a fraud loss of 10 basis points—1,000 of these accounts get compromised. Consider the following two models:

Model 1: At 20:1, AFPR identifies 40 percent of all fraud amounts and 25% of all compromised accounts.

Model 2: At 20:1, AFPR identifies 40 percent of all fraud amounts and 40 percent of all compromised accounts.

Which model is better? It seems intuitive as the detection rates are higher for Model 2. However, if we analyze the numbers and understand them, we might come to a different conclusion. Let's look at the numbers for each model.

Model 1 identifies 25 percent of all fraud accounts. This yields 25%*1000 = 250 fraud accounts. In order to understand the numbers behind 20:1 AFPR, multiply 250 by 20, which should give us the number of legitimate accounts identified by Model 1. This yields 250*20 = 5000 legitimate accounts. So, Model 1 will go through (5000 + 250) = 5250 accounts in order to identify 25% of the total fraud amount.

Model 2 identifies 40 percent of all fraud accounts. This yields 40%*1000 = 400 fraud accounts. In order to understand the numbers behind 20:1 AFPR, multiply 400 by 20, which should give us the number of legitimate accounts identified by Model 2. This yields 400*20 = 8000 legitimate accounts. So, Model 2 will go through (8000 + 400) = 8400 accounts in order to identify 40 percent of the total fraud amount.

In order to identify the same fraud dollar losses, Model 2 will require fraud operations to call an additional (8400 − 5250) = 3150 accounts. This will be a significant and totally hidden operational expense. This is because AFPR, the ratio of two quantities, hides the actual numbers behind the ratio.

Most fraud operations are run based on the outsort volume (the volume of transactions or accounts that operations will have to go through in order to detect a certain amount of fraud) that the operations can support. It would make logical sense to measure detection rates against outsort volume. When thus measured, a model with higher values for fraud account and fraud dollar loss detection rate is truly superior. While I believe measuring against outsort volume is a better indicator of fraud performance, measurement against AFPR is not without benefit. Measuring both fraud account and fraud dollar loss detection rates against AFPR ensure that there is a good balance between accounts and dollar losses detected by the system. In other words, we would like to make sure that the model detects not only enough fraud dollar loss, but also enough accounts with fraud loss.

Measuring both fraud account and fraud dollar loss detection rates against AFPR is crucial, but this measure cannot be used in isolation, and it cannot be the only measure used. Unfortunately, it is used all too often as the only measure. Even worse, account detection rate versus AFPR is used to compare models, and the models with the higher account detection are considered to be better. Based on the example above, it is very clear that such models would lead to higher volumes of accounts called and a higher good account annoyance.

UNSUPERVISED AND SEMISUPERVISED MODELING METHODOLOGIES

When dealing with fraud that is very sparse or with insufficient fraud history recorded, unsupervised and semisupervised modeling methodologies (as mentioned earlier in the book) are very useful. In unsupervised modeling, there is no available fraud information from the past. In semisupervised modeling, there is limited fraud information available from the past. It is essential to learn from the limited examples available and extrapolate how the portfolio is behaving today. Such processes require some level of understanding of how the model is working and what additional information can be provided to the model to improve its efficacy. The analytics experts and business experts have to work hand in hand to make this happen. It is important to learn from fraud successfully identified in the past as well as fraud that was completely missed because either the detection system failed to identify it correctly or the detection system didn't even target the fraud. We must learn from what worked in the past as well as from what we don't know about the past.

There are some interesting nonlinear techniques that can effectively deal with this problem, but significant leaps in fraud detection can be made only if the modelers work side by side with the fraud experts to understand and guide the modeling process. If the model identifies some entities as having been compromised, we must understand which ones are likely to be fraud and which ones were probably not compromised. This learning should be used to feed the modeling process and retrain the models to make them more accurate. Measuring these models will also require a lot of finesse as confirming fraud, especially for first-party fraud (fraud episodes where the person with the relationship with the bank is perpetrating the fraud), will be challenging and the information will have to be classified and understood correctly. It is a continuous cycle of learning, and when it is done well, this method provides rich results.

Hence, fraud model development is challenging, and so too is fraud model measurement. The better these ideas are understood by the entire organization, the better the organization will utilize the fraud detection system.

SUMMARY

Model performance measurement needs to be analyzed and understood in order for fraud departments to effectively use and monitor models in production. There are many nuances to this. With the pervasive nature of data science now (and this will only increase as we move into the future), it is not just the data scientists that need to deeply understand this but rather every single person in every team in the process. Continuously monitoring models in production and applying remedial measures as quickly as possible to any issues discovered are just as important as designing and implementing an excellent data-driven system.

CHAPTER **9**

The End: It Is Really the Beginning!

istory has witnessed many "Golden Age" periods. We are now entering the golden age of predictive analytics. The last several decades have been spent accumulating data meticulously. The race to make sense of this data is on. Being able to develop insight into the data gathered—from a historical context as well as a predictive context—is becoming the primary driver of many businesses.

As a statistician, I feel very gratified to live in this era. At the beginning of my career, I worked as a biostatistician and still remember vividly how lucky and happy I felt when a surgical experiment was conducted on 30 rats as opposed to 15 rats. At least we could pretend the law of large numbers was being used. Certain areas of biostatistics still have to rely on very little data to draw some key conclusions. It is the nature of clinical research, especially when the researchers are trying to establish a procedure as valid. It can be prohibitively expensive to conduct an experiment on a large number of specimens to establish validity. Once an idea is validated, a much broader set of subjects can be used for the research. In areas of research, the issue of having to use such limited data probably cannot be totally eliminated. However, behavioral modeling can be based on a lot more data today than was possible even ten years ago.

The capturing and storing of the data have become really inexpensive. Terabytes don't have to be "terror" bytes anymore. This opens up possibilities way beyond what we are used to. Quoting my favorite author, Stephen Covey, "Live out of your imagination, not your history"[1] is something that can be used very effectively in the field of analytics. I am not a big believer in using complex techniques just for the sake of it—I recommend using complex techniques only if they yield additional incremental value—but a number of predictive techniques are available today that didn't exist a decade ago, and they are going to help solve problems that no one has ever even attempted to solve.

Until very recently, I had witnessed a peculiar phenomenon across many institutions. The process of thoroughly understanding data used to be kept separate from the process of building the predictive models. But understanding the data is integral to any successful modeling project. When data mining emerged as an important discipline, awareness of the importance of data increased. The field of data science combines the functions of data extraction and understanding and the application of this knowledge to predictive models. The coming together of understanding the data and of using the data to build models is very exciting. I think this confluence is going to add significant value to solving very difficult problems. Curiosity about the data and a thorough knowledge of it is front, right, and center in addressing some of these problems. Curiosity and data science go together. Defining, understanding, and utilizing the data continuum are the most important ingredients in a successful modeling project, along with the sophistication of the modeling techniques. As we know, staying still in life is not possible. If we are not improving, we are going backward. Increasing the emphasis on data is certainly a way in which we can improve and move forward. Data provides reliable answers to a number of risk management problems today and will provide even more answers in the future.

As we embark on this exciting journey into the future, let us not forget that, while there are some universal truths that always hold true, many of today's assumptions will inevitably be broken tomorrow. Our flexibility to change these assumptions and the ability we exhibit to constantly question the status quo will shape our future. Eleanor Roosevelt once said, "I think, at a child's birth, if a mother could ask a fairy godmother to endow it with the most useful gift, that gift should be curiosity."[2] The gift of curiosity is what will define the future of analytics as well. The institutions that embrace curiosity, flexibility, and the ability to question the status quo will be the winners. I am reminded of what Walt Disney said: "We keep moving forward, opening new doors, and doing things, because we are curious and curiosity keeps leading us down new paths."[3] May financial institutions never lose their curiosity about data and what the data can teach us!

Notes

Chapter One—Bank Fraud: Then and Now

1. Alick R.W. Harrison, *The Law of Athens*, vol. 2 (Oxford University Press, 1971), page 114.

2. O. R. Krishnaswami, *The Wisdom of Thirukkural, A Guide to Living—A Commentary* (Bharatiya Vidya Bhavan, 2004).

3. http://en.wikipedia.org/wiki/Willie_Sutton

4. Antony St. Peter, *The Greatest Quotations of All-Time* (Xlibris, 2010), page 264.

5. Nassim Nicholas Taleb, *The Black Swan: The Impact of the Highly Improbable* (Penguin Books, 2008).

6. Terry Breverton, *Immortal Words: History's Most Memorable Quotations and the Stories behind Them* (Arcturus, 2009), page 16.

7. In Simon Singh, *The Code Book: The Science of Secrecy from Ancient Egypt to Quantum Cryptography* (Anchor, 2000).

Chapter Two—Quantifying Fraud: Whose Loss Is It Anyway?

1. http://techcrunch.com/2010/08/04/schmidt-data/

2. www.cmybacon.com/2012/01/1tb-swiss-army-knife-usb-flash-drive/

3. www.math.wpi.edu/Course_Materials/SAS/quotes.html

4. www.brainyquote.com/quotes/authors/p/philip_stanhope.html

5. Stanley J. Sienkiewicz, "Credit Cards and Payment Efficiency," August 2001. http://papers.ssrn.com/sol3/papers.cfm?abstract_id=927493

6. www.creditcards.com/credit-card-news/credit-cards-history-1264.php

7. George E.P. Box and Norman R. Draper, *Empirical Model-Building and Response Services* (John Wiley & Sons, 1987), page 424.

8. www.win.tue.nl/~adibucch/6BV04/tutorialTryggWold.pdf

Chapter Three—In God We Trust. The Rest Bring Data!

1. Arthur Conan Doyle, *Adventures of Sherlock Holmes* (Harper & Brothers, 1892), page 289.

2. Arthur Conan Doyle, *A Study in Scarlet* (Books on Demand, 2013), page 31.

3. Richard Steins, *Colin Powell: A Biography* (Greenwood, 2003), page 26.

4. Albert Van Helden, *Measuring the Universe* (University of Chicago Press, 1985), page 5.

5. Dava Sobel, *Galileo's Daughter* (Walker & Company, 1999), page 49.

6. Richard P. Feynman, *The Feynman Lectures on Physics*, vol. 1, (Dorling Kingersley, 2009), section 15-3.

7. Naomi Oreskes (ed.), *Plate Tectonics, An Insider's History of Modern Theory of the Earth* (Westview Group, 2003).

8. Manoranjan Kumar, *Dictionary of Quotations* (APH Publishing Corporation, 2008), page 66.

9. John R. Schermerhorn, Jr., *Introduction to Management*, International Student Version, 11th edition (John Wiley & Sons, 2011), page 360.

10. www.math.wpi.edu/Course_Materials/SAS/quotes.html

11. Written in 1895, first published in *Rewards and Fairies* (Macmillan and Co., 1910).

Chapter Four—Tackling Fraud: The Ten Commandments

1. Jay Abraham, *Getting Everything You Can Out of All You Have Got* (St. Martin's Press, 2000), page 3.

2. Stephen Covey, *The Seven Habits of Highly Effective People* (Simon & Schuster, 1989).

3. Charles Babbage, *Passages from the Life of a Philosopher* (Longman, Green, Longman, Roberts & Green, 1864), page 67.

4. William Shakespeare (author), J.A. Bryant and S. Barnet (eds.), *Romeo and Juliet*, revised edition (Signet Classics, 1998), act 2, scene 2.

5. Mitch Albom, *The Five People You Meet in Heaven* (Hyperion Books, 2003).

6. Larry Chang, *Wisdom for the Soul* (Gnosophia, 2006), page 473.

Chapter Five—It Is Not Real Progress Until It Is Operational

1. Richard J. Noyes and Pamela J. Robertson, *Guts in the Clutch: 77 Legendary Triumphs, Heartbreaks and Wild Finishes in 12 Sports* (Booksurge Publishing, 2009), page 83.

Chapter Eight—The Proof of the Pudding May Not Be in the Eating

1. This is not a quote of Leonardo da Vinci. It is attributed to Russell C. Taylor, in "The Joy of Service." www.lds.org/general-conference/1984/10/the-joy-of-service?lang=eng

2. This is not a quote of Leonardo da Vinci. It is attributed to William Gaddis in *The Recognitions* (Harcourt Brace and Company, 1955), page 457.

3. Robert Francis Harper, *The Code of Hammurabi, King of Babylon* (University of Chicago Press, 1904), section 229.

Chapter Nine—The End: It Is Really the Beginning!

1. Eric Allenbaugh, *Wake-Up Calls* (Simon and Schuster, 1994), page 65.

2. M.P. Sing, *Quote Unquote: A Handbook of Famous Quotations* (Lotus Press, 2006), page 95.

3. Jane Sutcliff, *Walt Disney* (Lerner Publications, 2009), page 45.

Index

A

Abraham, Jay, 65
account behavior, deviations in, 82
account take-over fraud, 70
ACH. *See* automated clearing house (ACH)
acquisition/merger, 53
address change, 84
"The Adventures of Copper Beeches" (Doyle), 39
advertisement monetization, 13
after-death experience, 85
air disaster risk, 64–65
Albom, Mitch, 85
American Express, 24, 26, 29
American Express cards, 26
analytical fraud management process, 71
analytics for fraud management, 89
analytics teams, 90
analytics-based scoring system, 96
anomalies in data, 55, 76
application transactions, 92
approve-or-decline decision, 12
Aristarchus of Samos, 41
assets to pay back a loan, 4
ATM terminal, 18, 27, 33, 82
ATM withdrawals, 18, 33, 68–69, 82
authenticating customer's identity, 28
authentication, 8, 106
    methods, 5, 30
    protocols, 27
    system, 70
authorization transactions, 20
automated clearing house (ACH), 20, 97, 112
automated predictive dialers, 101
average transaction amount, 125
averaging approach, 105
avgMCCrsk, 126
avgPOSrsk, 126

B

Babbage, Charles, 67
balance inquiry transaction, 69

Bank of America, 24
BankAmerica Service Corporation, 25
bank-developed rules, 91
bankruptcy, 19, 93
basis point (BP), 95
behavioral
    input, 7
    modeling, 5, 13, 17, 33, 42, 45–46, 162
    models, 43, 46, 56, 60
behavior-based models, 28
behavior-based segments, 79
"below the radar," 122
Berra, Yogi (American baseball catcher), 6
Biggins, John (banker), 24
BIN number, 29
biostatistician, 42, 161
Black Swan (Taleb), 6
BP. *See* basis point (BP)
Brahe, Tycho, 41

C

card authorizations, 50
card fraud, 95
cardholder's behavior, 5, 32
cardholder's monthly statement, 19
card-not-present fraud, 28, 99
card-not-present transaction, 50
card-present transaction, 50
cash deposits, 6
cash users, 81–82
cash withdrawals, 6, 27, 92
casual fraud, 83
cat and mouse game, 122
causal relationships, 41–42
central limit theorem (CLT), 43
change monitoring, 73
"Charge-It" card, 24
charge-off risk, 19
charitable organization donation, 29
checking account fraud, 70
chip card, 50

Churchill, Winston, 55
Clark, Frank A., 86
closed-loop system, 24
cloud computing, 74
CLT. *See* central limit theorem (CLT)
coin flipping, 95
competitive advantage, 51–52
conditional probability, 65
conditional risk, 64–65
confidence intervals, 7
consortium-based models,
    112–13
consumer expectations, 79
consumer exposure, 9
Copernicus, 41
counterfeit card fraud, 29
Covey, Stephen, 65, 162
credit
   limit, 26
   line, unspent, 9
   risk, 19, 30–31, 36, 66, 76, 91, 93,
     95, 101
   risk losses, 9
   risk management, 36
credit card(s), 4, 10, 25
   affiliated with Visa and MasterCard, 25
   fraud, 9–10, 23, 30–31
   fraud losses, 12
   high interest rates on, 4
   offers, 11
   portfolios, 4–5, 19, 25–26
   system, national, 24
   thefts, 19, 27
   transactions, 12
"Credit Card and Payment Efficiency"
   (Sienkiewicz), 23
cryptographic messages, 13
cryptography, 13
customer
   acquisition, 3
   annoyance, 79, 100
   behavior based on past history, 5
   complains about fraud, 21
   expectation, 44–46
   insight, 13
   level information, 57
   service, 22, 30, 89
   touchpoint, 13
customer's identity, authenticating, 28
cyber-attacks, 106
cycle of improvement, 88

D
Da Vinci, Leonardo, 153
data
   analysis, 6, 13, 91, 119
   anomalies, 112
   anomalies in, 55
   assets, 48, 52–53, 75
   associated, 17
   for behavioral models, 46–47
   changes, 51, 55
   collection, 42
   field changes, 71, 112
   handling, 119
   mapping, 73
   mining, 100–101
   from "monetary" transactions, 68
   proliferation, 40
   science, 109, 162
   storage, 16
   streams, 51
   warehouses, 55, 71, 74, 103–4
data environment, 73
   1. know your data, 47–48
   2. collect all data you can from day
     one, 47–51
   3. allow for additions as the data
     grows, 47, 51–52
   4. if you cannot integrate the
     data, you cannot integrate the
     businesses, 47, 52–53
   5. when you change the definition
     of a field, it is best to augment and
     not modify, 47, 53–54
   6. document data you have as well
     as the data you lost, 47, 54
   7. when change happens, document
     it, 47, 55
   8. ETL: "extract, translate, load" (not
     "extract, taint, lose"), 47, 55–56
   9. data model is an impressionist
     painting, 47, 56–57
   10. top two assets of any business
     are people and data, 47, 57–58
database storage, 52
data-checking processes, 17
data-driven
   decisions, 50
   environment, 50
   fraud detection systems, 13
   fraud management system, 91,
     110–12, 110 f6.1

highend analytical system, 90
organization, 75
predictive modeling, 39
risk management, 37–38, 68
system to combat fraud, 20
techniques, 55
debit card
fraud, 23, 30–31, 70
number, 69
silo point of view, 70
transactions, 12
decision keys, 35
defined fields, repurposing, 72
dichotomous variable, 124
Diner's Club cards, 24
Disney, Walt, 163
Disraeli, Benjamin (Prime Minister), 7
dollars at risk, 66
domain expertise, 40
domain experts, 100, 103
domestic wire, 20
Doyle, Arthur Conan (author), 39–40
Dulany, Paul, 22

E

eCommerce transactions, 28
economies of scale, 25
Einstein, Albert, 149
electronic goods, 10
electronic store purchases, 10–11
end-to-end monitoring, 117
enterprise fraud management, 71
enterprise fraud modeling, 70
entropy of system, 73–74
ether theory, 41
expiration date on card, 29
extract, translate, load (ETL), 55–56

F

face-to-face interactions, 3
false positive(s), 122
rate, 66
ratio, 99, 102, 116, 155–56
transactions, 78
field definition, 54, 75
field documentation, 72
financial forecasting, 76
financial institutions, 3
financial marketplace consolidation, 52
First Data Corporation, 25
first-party fraud, 21, 159

Fisher, Ronald Aylmer, 60
fraud
analysis, evolution of, 8–9
analyst, "smile and dial," 84, 99
analysts, 35, 83, 86, 94, 101, 104
automated process of detecting, 5
banks are vulnerable to, 3
card-not-present, 28
control results, 89
control systems, 87
data, accurate, 36–37
departments, 9
detection, 14
detection performance, 79, 82, 122
detection solutions, 153
detection systems, 2, 13, 19–21, 32,
    34–36, 68, 82, 84, 86, 88, 90, 93,
    96, 98, 100, 102, 107
detection techniques, 34
episodes, 18–20, 36, 70, 80, 82, 84,
    92, 94, 97, 102, 156, 159
evolution of, 2
experts, 10
in financial institutions, 19
in Hindu mythology, 2
losses, 22, 26, 31, 154–56
lost-and-stolen, 28
management, 46, 153–56
management departments, 65, 78
management exercise, 77
management groups, 88
management in banks, 22–23
management infrastructure, 90
management mindset, 85
management of credit cards, 22–23,
    29, 32, 34–37
management system data-driven, 91,
    110–12, 110 f6.1
management systems, 83, 89,
    91, 104
management units, 86
managers, 66, 86, 122
oldest case of, 2
operations analysts, 96
in a particular zip code, 103
pattern, 154
in present day, 2–3
rate, 124–25, 150
risk, 6, 12, 19, 22, 30, 35, 64, 66–67,
    81–82, 91, 95
risk management, 66

fraud(*continued*)
  rules, 77–78
  score, 35, 79, 83–84
  scoring systems, 7
  stigma associated with, 2
  strategies, 31, 50, 94, 100–101,
    103–5
  strategy development, 116
  time-sensitive nature of, 101
  transactions, 123–24
fraud analytics, 121
  data, 126, 128
  data, note about, 125–26
  logistic regression 1, 132, 132t7.9,
    133t7.18
  logistic regression 2, 136–37
  logistic regression 3, 141–43
  logistic regression 4, 145–47
  neural network 1, 134, 135t7.19,
    135t7.21
  neural network 2, 138–39
  neural network 3, 143–44
  neural network 4, 147–48
  probability of detection *versus*
    probability of false alarm, 123f7.1
  regression 1, 128, 131t7.5, 131t7.8
  regression 2, 134–36
  regression 3, 140
  regression 4, 144–45
  SAS system, 127t7.1
  statistics, 128
fraud metrics, 86
fraud model, essentials of
  building a, 112
fraud model performance, 98, 154
fraud models, challenges in
  operationalizing
  1. operations personnel need to
    understand the fraud score
    concept, 94–98
  2. score development process must
    consider operational use and
    constraints, 94, 98–101
  3. fraud strategies should
    complement and not compete
    with the fraud score, 94, 101–4
  4. fraud strategies and operational
    processes should be well
    documented, 94, 104–5
fraud-related decisions, 45
fraudsters

  anonymity of, 3
  prefer night-time, 10
  sophisticated, 3, 87
  use loopholes in the system, 71
fraudulent
  application, 31, 98, 101, 104
  behavior, 21, 37
  patterns, 5
  purchases, 27
  transactions, 19–20, 37
frontline employees, 118

G
Gaddis, William, 153
Gerson, Emily Starbuck, 24
goal setting, 86
Goodnight, Jim (CEO), 57
governance requirements, 91
granular data, 49–50
granularity in classification, 52

H
Hades (God of death), 23
Hammurabi (Babylonian ruler), 155
Hegestratos, 1–3
high-throughput environment, 115
historical data, 112
historical transactional data, 92
"The History of Credit Cards" (Woolsey
  and Gerson), 24
Holmes, Sherlock, 39

I
ID theft, 20, 33
identity, your, 9
"If" (Kipling), 60–61
impressionist paintings, 56–57
insurance money, 1
intelligent systems, 58
InterBank Card Association, 25
interchange revenue, 11
internal fraud, 112
international wire, 20
Internet data, 59
Internet merchants, 28
Internet pop-up ads, 44
Internet shopping, 29
Internet site, anomalous activity at, 34
intrusive questions at website, 28
intuition, 64
IP addresses, 106

The Five People You Meet in Heaven
    (Albom), 85

K

key business problems, 51
key field information, 73
Kipling, Rudyard, 60
"kitchen sink" model, 78
knowledge-based businesses, 58

L

laws of thermodynamics, 73
"lies; damned lies; and statistics," 7
life cycle of customer's bank
    dealings, 85
life cycle of data, 85
linear regression models, 80, 122,
    124, 136
linear statistical models, 46
logistic regression, 124, 126, 128,
    148–50
    regression 1, 132, 132t7.9, 133t7.18
    regression 2, 136–37
    regression 3, 141–43
    regression 4, 145–47
lost-and-stolen fraud, 28, 99
low credit risk, 111

M

magnetic stripe on card, 29, 50
*Manuscript on Deciphering Cryptographic
    Messages*
    (Al-Kindi), 13
marketing-related decisions, 45
MasterCard, 25–26, 28–29
mathematical algorithm, 6
MCC codes, 125–26
MCC risk, 126
merchant category code, 77
metadata layers, 49, 71, 74
Michelson and Morley experiment, 41
Mid-America Bankcard Association, 25
mini statement, 69–71
missing data, 54, 71, 76
mobile channel, 60
model performance measurement, 94
model score, 35, 100
model suite implementation, 116–17
model-based systems, 78, 80
modeling, advanced, 76
modeling algorithms, 124

"Models should be as simple as
    possible, but not simpler," 149–51
monetary damage, 40
monetary losses, 94–95
money lending, 3
monitoring and fined tuning, 115–16
multi-entity behavioral modeling, 33
multiple entities in real time, 83

N

national credit card system, 24
network intrusion, 34, 112
network–based behavior models, 12
neural network
    about, 30, 78–79, 124–26, 128, 134,
        149–50
    back propagation, 81
    models, nonlinear behavior–based, 30
    network 1, 134, 135t7.19, 135t7.21
    network 2, 138–39
    network 3, 143–44
    network 4, 147–48
new data feeds, 87
New York's Franklin National Bank, 24
"no one is indispensable," 75
non–cash users, 81
non-fraud transactions, 78
nonlinear models, 46, 78, 124
nonlinear statistical models, 11–13
nonlinear techniques, 158
non-monetary transactions, 69–70
normal behavior of customers,
    17–18

O

odd behavior, 5
Ohnstad, Mitch (reporter), 3
open-loop system, 25
operational processes and
    constraints, 101
operational rule, 154
originator–beneficiary combination, 33
"out of character" transaction, 82
over-limit approval decisions, 91

P

Passages from the Life of a Philosopher
    (Babbage), 67
password, 5, 28
past information, 104
perceived risk, 64

personal information, 44
phone number change, 84
PIN number, 69, 82, 84, 93, 106, 109
point of sale (POS), 12, 69, 97, 107, 125
   codes, 125–26
   risk, 126
Powell, Colin (General), 40
predictive (detection) analytics, 121
predictive modeling, 17, 39, 50
predictive models, 17
premier customers, 98
process improvement, 86
production monitoring of data, 68
Protos, 1
proxy documentation, 72
Ptolemy's theory, 41
purchase behavior, abnormal, 34

Q
quality checks of data, 50
quality control, 155
quantifiable losses, 93
quantifying fraud
   accurate data, importance of, 22
   behavioral models, 30–31
   credit cards, 23–26
   data storage and statistical thinking,
      16–17
   fraud, card-not-present, 28–29
   fraud, lost-and-stolen, 26–28
   fraud detection, using it effectively,
      35–37
   fraud detection across domains,
      33–34
   fraud episode, recording the, 19–21
   fraud in credit card industry, 22–23
   fraud management, 31–33
   modeling, supervised vs.
      unsupervised, 21–22
   non-fraud behavior, understanding,
      17–18
   potential risk, quantifying, 18–19

R
rank-ordering tool, 102
reason codes, 103, 104
recording frauds, 21
regression 1, 128, 131t7.5, 131t7.8
regression 2, 134–36
regression 3, 140
regression 4, 144–45

regulatory scrutiny, 101
right attitude, 117–19
rip-and-replace policy, 119
risk calculation, 59
risk management, 7, 14
risk management systems, 88
risk/reward equation, 4
Roosevelt, Eleanor, 163
rules-based systems, 78–80, 90, 102
Russell, Bill (basketball player), 90
Russian IP address, 106

S
SAS system, 127t7.1
Schmidt, Eric (Google), 16
score algorithms, 59
score-based queues, 96
scoring processes, 83
scoring systems, 59, 80, 82, 86, 96
seasonality of fraud episodes, 92
second law of thermodynamics, 73
secured lending, 4–5, 9, 12–13, 20
security questions, 28
semi-supervised modeling, 21, 158
The Seven Habits of Highly Effective People
   (Covey), 65
Shewart, Walter (Bell Labs
   physicist), 155
Sienkiewicz, Stan (Federal Reserve
   Bank of Philadelphia), 23
signatures, 9
Sisyphus, King, 23
skimmed data, 82
skimmed debit card, 70
skimming, 27, 82
small-dollar charges, 10
sourcing the account, 111
spending limits, 9, 84
standards of privacy, 44
Stanhope, Philip (British statesman), 18
statistical modeling, 6–7
statistical models, 6–8, 11
statistical thinking, 16–17
statistics, 128
supervised modeling, 21
supply chain management, 109
Sutton, Willie (bank robber), 3

T
Taj Mahal, 46
Taleb, Nassim Nicholas (author), 6

target- based modeling, 21
Taylor, Russell C., 153
ten commandments of fraud
    management
  1. garbage in; garbage out, 67–71
  2. no documentation? no change,
     67, 71–75
  3. key employees are not a substitute
     for good documentation, 67,
     75–77
  4. rules: more doesn't mean better,
     67, 77–79
  5. score: never rest on your laurels,
     67, 79–83
  6. score + rules = winning strategy,
     67, 83–85
  7. fraud is everyone's problem, 67,
     85–86
  8. continual assessment is the key,
     67, 86–87
  9. fraud control systems: if they rest,
     they rust, 67, 87–88
  10. continual improvement: the
      cycle never ends, 67, 88
text data, 58–60
text-mining algorithms, 59
thin-client access, 74
third-party fraud, 21
Thiruvalluvar (poet), 2
3D Secure protocol, 28
"time-on-books," 53

"time-since-first-transaction," 53
transaction(al)
    amount, 125
    dates, 125
    details, 92
    information, 92
    times, 125
    zero monetary loss, 93
traveler's checks, 24

U
unsecured lending, 4–5, 9,
    12–13
unsecured loan, 4
U.S. Postal Service, 24

V
verification calls, 102
"Verified by Visa," 27
video camera at ATM, 27, 69
Visa, 25–29

W
Wallis, Lynn, 113–14
Wells, H. G., 17
wire fraud, 112
withdrawal transaction, 17
Woolsey, Ben, 24

X
Xenothemis, 1–2

9 780470 494394